Zadie Smith's
White Teeth

CONTINUUM CONTEMPORARIES

Also available in this series

Forthcoming in this series

· **ZADIE SMITH'S**

White Teeth

A READER'S GUIDE

CLAIRE SQUIRES

CONTINUUM | NEW YORK | LONDON

2007

The Continuum International Publishing Group Inc
80 Maiden Lane, New York, NY 10038

The Continuum International Publishing Group Ltd
The Tower Building, 11 York Road, London SE1 7NX

www.continuumbooks.com

Printed in the United States of America

Library of Congress Cataloging-in-Publication Data

Squires, Claire.
    Zadie Smith's White teeth : a reader's guide / Claire Squires
        p. cm. — (Continuum contemporaries)
    Includes bibliographical references.
    ISBN 0-8264-5326-0 (alk. paper)
    1. Smith, Zadie. White teeth. 2. London (england) — In literature. 3.
West Indians in literature. I. Smith, Zadie. White teeth. II. Title.
III. Series.
PR6069.M59 W4737 2002
823'.914 — dc21
                            2002000884

Contents

Acknowledgments

With many thanks to everyone who has shared their opinions on *White Teeth* with me, and listened to mine. My particular thanks go the Oxford Contemporary Writing Reading Group, Caroline Davis's reading group, Borders Charing Cross Road reading group, Penny Fryer and her Upper Sixth Form class at Latymer Upper School, David Barker at Continuum, Sophy Dale (for the mutual support), Rosie Holland, Julia Reid, Chloë Evans, and my parents.

1

The Novelist

"What's past is prologue": this quotation from Shakespeare's play *The Tempest* serves as epigraph to Zadie Smith's first novel, *White Teeth* (2000). It declares the importance of the pre-history of her characters, the legacy of their origins and the question of how they arrived at the present, immediately giving a frame to the tale that she is about to tell. And as it is in her fiction, so it is in her life.

Smith was born on October 27, 1975 in northwest London, the area that she grew up in and continues to inhabit. The racially-mixed and largely working-class London borough of Brent, with its communities of Willesden Green, Cricklewood and Kilburn, also provides the back-drop to *White Teeth*. A sprawling saga of several generations that spans the twentieth century, the novel's characters travel to and from Bangladesh, Bulgaria, Jamaica, Italy, and Scandinavia, but all congregate in the streets of Smith's London. The three families around which the plot weaves—the British and Jamaican Joneses, the Bangladeshi Iqbals, and the Jewish Catholic Chalfens—live within a short distance of each other, and their common geographical location overrides their disparate heritage to link their destinies. On its publication at the beginning of 2000, *White Teeth* was widely praised by the critics as a celebration of multicultural London, and has become one of the bestselling and most critically acclaimed first novels of recent years, a feat accomplished by an author in her early twenties.

Smith was born to a black Jamaican mother and a white English father. Her mother grew up in Jamaica, remaining there with her grandmother when her own mother emigrated to England, only joining her on the death of her grandmother in 1969. She attended two final years of school in England before working as a typist, model and eventually social worker and child psychologist. Smith's father, a photographer for direct mail and advertising companies, had been previously married before starting a new family with her mother. Her parents divorced when Smith was a teenager. With her two younger brothers, she continued to live with her mother in London, only moving out after the success of *White Teeth* allowed her to purchase her own flat in Kilburn, not far from the family home.

Smith attended local state schools, including Hampstead Comprehensive, a secondary school whose intake reflected the multicultural aspect of the borough in which it is located. Hampstead Comprehensive serves as a model for Glenard Oak, the school attended by Irie and her generation in the 1980s and 1990s sections of *White Teeth*. This is the same period that Smith was at secondary school, and while the fictional Glenard Oak is not a direct portrayal of Hampstead Comprehensive, it is one of the synchronies between Smith's life and her novel. In interview, however, Smith has been cautious to accept a description of her writing as autobiographical. Indeed, *White Teeth* is anything but a narrowly-focused bildungsroman. Its reach extends to different races, religions, generations and genders, although adolescent angst also has its place in her writing. At a time when many other young novelists were perceived to be shying away from large issues for a more introverted form of fiction, the broad vision of *White Teeth* has undoubtedly contributed to its warm reception. Nonetheless, there are similarities between Smith's own life and aspects of her characters: notably in her mixed-race parentage; in being the progeny of an older father and a younger mother; and in the Willesden Green location. It is worth bearing in mind that Irie, the character whom many critics found to be the most sympathetically drawn, shares Smith's demographic almost exactly.

While Smith denies that her characters are direct portraits of her own experience, she makes it clear that details of her autobiography have contributed to the themes of *White Teeth*, as she explained to the *Observer*'s interviewer Stephanie Merritt, "'*White Teeth* is not really based on personal family experience [. . .] When you come from a mixed-race family, it makes you think a bit harder about inheritance and what's passed on from generation to generation. But as for racial tensions — I'm sure my parents had the usual trouble getting hotel rooms and so on, but I don't talk to them much about that part of their lives.'" The themes of inheritance are, as this comment suggests, prominent in the novel, and so although there may not be a simple transcription of real-life person as *White Teeth* character, autobiography is of relevance.

Where Smith does readily accept an autobiographical slant to her work is in its topography. In interview with Christina Patterson of the *Independent*, she said, "'If there's anything autobiographical in it [. . .] then it's Willesden Green, rather than any of the people in the book.'" Willesden Green and its abutting suburbs are an area relatively unhymned either in literature or by estate agents. It has also evaded the spotlight shone on London districts such as Brixton, Notting Hill, and Hackney, notorious in past decades for their racial tensions and riots, and latterly celebrated for the vibrancy and local color lent to them by their immigrant communities. One measure of *White Teeth*'s ascendancy in the public consciousness is made by the London *Evening Standard* running an article about the new desirability of the hitherto anonymous postcode of NW2: "Cheap, cosmopolitan, and 20 minutes from the centre of town on the Jubilee Line, it's a place where you can buy a bagel, a patty, a curry and a bodhran in the same parade of shops." This is multiculturalism as style guide, in no small part influenced by the success of *White Teeth*. Another measure of the book's rise, though, is in the textual plaudits offered to Smith for her portrayal of this small segment of multicultural London, the place described by Michiko Kakutani's *New York Times* review of the novel as "a cacophonous, Martin Amis-ish London of curry shops and pool halls and cheap hair salons."

Kakutani's review stresses that Smith's London is not solely transcribed from the streets, but also draws on the literary tradition of near contemporaries, such as Amis, but also of earlier accounts of the capital, pre-eminently Charles Dickens's. The question of literary influence came to play a crucial influence in the critics' response to *White Teeth*, a question that was contested by Smith in her analysis of the role that marketing and ethnicity plays in the interpretation of texts. Despite her disavowals, though, Smith is without doubt a *reader*. When asked whether writing can be taught through creative writing classes, her negative response emphasized instead the importance of writers as readers: "The best, the only real training you can get is from reading other people's books." This assertion suggests that a literary education plays a crucial, if not always direct, role in her fiction.

After leaving school, Smith became the first member of her family to go to university, gaining a place at King's College, Cambridge. Studying for a degree in English Literature she provided herself with an intense training in "other people's books," a literary education whose results began to appear in the form of short stories published in university magazines. She published stories in the May Anthologies (collections of Cambridge and Oxford student writing) in the three years she was at university. She has dismissed these early efforts as pastiche, describing them in interview as "'one really bad Virginia Woolf, then one really bad Jeanette Winterson and one really bad Hanif Kureishi.'" To Smith's list should also be added Vladimir Nabokov, as one of the stories, "Picnic, Lightning," is prefaced with Smith's "apologies" to the author. Yet despite Smith's modest assertions, the stories "Mirrored Box" (1995), "The Newspaper Man" (1996), "Mrs Begum's Son and the Private Tutor" (1997), and "Picnic, Lightning" (1997), already display an author at ease with a range of voices and styles, depicting characters as varied as an upper-middle class, middle-aged woman left by her MP husband for his secretary, a young Oxford graduate making his way as a private tutor and would-be writer, and a 10-year-old Bangladeshi boy-cum-guru. It is particularly in the story "Mrs. Begum's Son and the Private Tutor," in which the latter two characters appear, that the themes and style of *White Teeth* are developed, and that Smith's portrayal of the streets of Willesden Green begins to take the shape her first novel would assume.

Smith may have dismissed "Mrs. Begum's Son and the Private Tutor" as a "really bad Hanif Kureishi" pastiche, but it is worth considering, not least for the links it has to her first novel. The story is narrated by Alex Pembrose, the graduate, who supports himself and his girlfriend by working as a private tutor in Willesden Green. The ethnic, religious and cultural mix of his students reflects the diverse nature of the area: Jews, Muslims, Hindus, and Christians, from Bangladesh, Pakistan, and Romania. Pembrose, on his autumnal walks to work, daydreams of meetings between his charges, and the intellectual, emotional, and cultural advantages he thinks might ensue:

I often wondered what would issue from a friendship between Parjev and Magid. During the leaf-kicking I played out scenarios for all my tutees — if, if, if this were not London and people's lives intersected as easily as their roads.

Over the course of the story, the geography of Willesden Green roads does come to be replayed through the intersection of people's lives. These intersections are brought about through a combination of satirically-portrayed local politics and the figure of the semi-mystical Magid. Pembrose is summoned by Magid's mother, Alsana Begum, to provide lessons and act as a companion to the child prodigy. Their lives are thrown together with other Brent inhabitants one day when they get caught up in a political demonstration. The demonstration is directed against the local council, who have taken the controversial decision not to allow an old bingo hall to be converted into an Asian community center. Smith describes the assembled interest groups in broad comic brushstrokes, as the multicultural diversity of the borough threatens to descend into a riot of rival voices:

On the other side of the square were young men with fledgling beards and big trousers giving out leaflets which said: *Khalifah. Learn about the ideal Islamic State.* There was a mime artist leading some children around a telephone box. The Asian Women's Community Action group turned up, and heckled, which brought more people, until there was quite a hefty crowd and Magid was squeezed between me and a fat lady.

The Liberal said something about the rainbow borough of Brent. A Rasta-woman with her front teeth missing sucked the rest of them in contempt. "Where's the colour in the council?" she said, and the crowd laughed. The red, yellow and blue men, pushed their pink fingertips deeper into their gloves and began again. Megaphone, drone, drone, cough, conclusion.

Magid goes missing amongst this cacophonous gathering, but as his tutor's increasingly frantic search for him unfolds, so Magid reappears: on the politicians' platform. He begins to speak, and first stills, and then silences, the crowd, even those who cannot understand his Bengali words. His oration shames the politicians into changing their decision, the rival interest groups are, at least momentarily, united, and Magid himself is hailed as a local guru. The newspapers besiege his front door, though what it was that Magid actually said to the crowd is lost in the general excitement and the centrality of the moment is muffled, its mystical overtones diffused.

"Mrs. Begum's Son and the Private Tutor" introduces many of the themes and, in slightly different form, some of the characters of *White Teeth*. Begum is the maiden name of *White Teeth's* Alsana Iqbal. In the short story she has two sons (though not twins), Magid and the self-named "Mark," Magid's anglicized, ladykiller of a brother who displays an interest in the Islamic fundamentalist group at the demonstration. Magid's vague explanation to Pembrose of what he said to the crowd — "'I just said . . . you know, that people should love and stuff . . . we should all mix together, Hindu, Muslim . . . I said everything could be so much *nicer* . . . the usual.'" — will later find its echo in Archie Jones's woolly vision of racial harmony: "You know, why couldn't people just get on with things, just live together, you know, in peace or harmony or something" (p. 194). Smith's representation of the multiple identities inhabiting her native Willesden Green sets the scene for *White Teeth's* stories of origins, roots, and cultures. Smith also finds a tone in which she will deal with the complex issues of her fiction: one that is comic, sympathetic, and — essentially — optimistic.

Although Smith entertained ambitions of becoming a journalist, her plans were changed when a publisher contacted her after reading her work in the May Anthologies. The publisher expressed interest in publishing a novel if she were writing one and, according to media report, offered in the region of £2,000 to her for doing so. A friend, however, recommended that if she were to write a novel, she should acquire a literary agent to represent her work. So, after starting work on the novel that would become *White Teeth*, she approached The Wylie Agency, an international group who represent a high-profile literary clientele including, among others, Salman Rushdie, Martin Amis, and Philip Roth. The Wylie Agency agreed to take Smith on as a client and so, while studying for her final examinations in Cambridge (for which she gained a first), she wrote the first chapters of the novel.

Smith's agents decided to sell her novel before it was completed. On the basis of a partial script of around eighty pages, they approached various publishers. A heated auction for the rights ensued in 1997, with Hamish Hamilton—who were not the original publisher who had approached Smith—emerging triumphant. Details of the advance deal, which was widely reported in the media, have not been officially confirmed, but have frequently been put at the level of £250,000 for two novels. Because of this reputedly high advance level, Smith's youth, and also her ethnic origins, attention was already attracted to *White Teeth* before it had even been written. The *Daily Telegraph*, *The Times*, and the *Independent* all mentioned Smith in December 1997 and January 1998 in various articles. During the period in which Smith was actually writing the rest of the novel, then, she had already come to public attention.

Before the novel was published, Smith's writing was showcased in major literary magazines on both sides of the Atlantic. An extract from the novel was published in the Autumn 1999 issue of *Granta*, and a short story, "Stuart", made its way into *The New Yorker's* "Millennial Fiction" issue at the turn of 1999/2000. Smith's literary reputation was established by her appearance in such prestigious arenas. Salman Rushdie, having read an advance copy of the novel, contributed a very positive endorsement of the book. When the novel was eventually published (in January 2000 in the U.K. and April 2000 in the U.S.), substantial marketing campaigns ensured widespread media coverage. The novel went on to win several prizes, including the Whitbread First Novel Award and the Commonwealth Writers Best First Book Prize, to be published in translation around the world, and to find a long-lived position in the bestseller lists, both in hardback and paperback editions.

The question of influence returns to any analysis of the review coverage of *White Teeth*, particularly in the assessment it makes of Smith's status as a multicultural writer. The expression "multicultural writer" suggests a double definition, referring to Smith both as an author with a mixed-race background, and as an author who writes *about* multiculturalism. Much of the media interest in Smith demonstrates a fascination with details of her background, making her, as one journalist rather euphemistically put it, "ethnically interesting." Such dubious blandishments aside, though, it is clear that Smith was a marketing department's dream: young, intelligent, attractive, and opinionated, and representative of multicultural Britain. As one journalist put it, "Zadie Smith is the perfect package for a literary marketing exercise," while another wrote that, "she ha[s] the fortune, or misfortune, to be the perfect demographic." When the British census of 2001 announced its extended categories for mixed-race Britons, Smith was mentioned in reports of the official announcement as an example of changing British demographics. As a media personality, then, Smith was taken as a symbol of a new Britain's self-definitions. Details of her biography, while not utterly dictating the terms of her first novel's reception, certainly increased her exposure.

Smith's position as a writer *about* multicultural society is a more complex issue, revealing the conjunction of publishers' marketing and the author's literary influences. Robert McCrum, reviewing the year's publications in the *Observer* at the end of 2000, commented of *White Teeth* that, "It's perhaps too early to say exactly how good this novel is, but there's no doubt that it marks an important literary watershed in much the same way as the publication of *Midnight's Children* or *The Buddha of Suburbia*. Certainly, Smith has been influenced by Rushdie and Kureishi, but she is triumphantly original and unquestionably a new writer to watch closely." In so doing, he summons two writers already seen to be of importance to Smith's career: Rushdie in providing an endorsement for her novel; and Kureishi for suggesting a model for the short story from which *White Teeth* developed. But in what ways, and to what extent, might these two writers be said to have influenced Smith, and why, as with her rejection of autobiographical readings of her work, has Smith come to deny such influences?

The greatest influence that Rushdie may have had on Zadie Smith is linguistic. While Rushdie's novel *Midnight's Children* (1981), repeatedly cited as a model for *White Teeth*, is also a multi-generational tale mingling ethnic origins, faiths, and families, Rushdie's is a novel of postcolonial India, whilst Smith's is of post-imperial London. There are structural similarities between the two novels, inasmuch as both have complex and occasionally non-realist plots, but these are recurrent traits of the postmodern novel, rather than a specific indication of Smith's allegiance to Rushdie. In the realm of language use, however, the debt Smith owes to Rushdie is more readily apparent. The playful register of Smith's coinages are, in their rhythmic cadences and combination of cultural provenance, reminiscent of the energetic Bombay street slang of Rushdie's characters, and his technique of creating neologisms by running words together. In *White Teeth*, for example, Alsana mocks her husband's portentous pronouncements about the fall of the Berlin Wall with a string of phrases redolent of an earlier England than their own:

"And who does he think he is? Mr Churchill-gee?" laughed Alsana scorn-fully. "Original whitecliffsdover piesnmash jellyeels royalvariety british-bulldog, heh?" (p. 241)

Such compound nouns, however, are also a legacy from Lewis Carroll, a writer whom Smith acknowledges as an influence in her introduction to an edition of *Through the Looking-Glass and What Alice Found There* (2001). Smith also adds London youth slang to her lexicon, in the "hybrid" language of Millat's "*Raggastani*" street crew, a "strange mix of Jamaican patois, Bengali, Gujarati and English" (p. 231).

The plotting of *White Teeth* also occasionally resembles elements of Rushdie's oeuvre, most specifically in its touches of magic realism. Millat breaking his nose in repetition of his twin is a moment both comic and saturated with meaning, a coincidence that also has its base in cause and effect. A string of other coincidences marks their bound lives, culminating in Magid's miraculous escape from a tornado and Millat's from HIV.

A more legitimate comparison of Rushdie's work to Smith's is not to be found in *Midnight's Children*, however, but in *The Satanic Verses* (1988). While Rushdie's earlier major novels, *Midnight's Children* and *Shame* (1983) focus on India and Pakistan, *The Satanic Verses* concentrates on a metropolitan centre of the old imperial world, London. For, as the critic Homi Bhabha has put it in *The Location of Culture* (1994), with specific regard to *The Satanic Verses* (but with general application to postcolonial novels based in the old imperial centers):

it is to the city that the migrants, the minorities, the diasporic come to change the history of the nation [. . .] it is the city which provides the space in which emergent identifications and new social movements of the people are played out. It is there that, in our time, the perplexity of the living is most acutely experienced.

The Satanic Verses provides a rich portrait of the immigrant communities of "Ellowen Deeowen": London. Its vision is more apocalyptic, more tense, and more surreal than the London of Smith's *White Teeth*, but the comparison is productive. Moreover, Smith inserts *The Satanic Verses* into her own text, in a sequence where Millat and his friends travel in January 1989 to the north of England to take part in an anti-book demonstration. Although Smith does not name the book nor the author, the parallels to *The Satanic Verses* affair — which saw some British Muslims protesting against the novel's perceived blasphemy by burning copies on the street — are apparent. Smith's insertion into her narrative of "one of the most significant events in modern British life," as the cultural commentator Yasmin Alibhai-Brown has termed it, both confirms her negotiation with Rushdie and his work, and the links between her writing and other recent fictionalized inscriptions of *The Satanic Verses* affair, including Hanif Kureishi's *The Black Album* (1995) and David Caute's *Fatima's Scarf* (1998). Yet in interview Smith has come to deny any similarity between her own writing and that of Rushdie and Kureishi. Despite affirming that Rushdie and Kureishi were "heroes of mine" in 1998, by the time of publication in 2000 Smith was saying that:

"I think some writers, not just me, feel that you're being compared to Rushdie or Kureishi just because there are Asian characters in your book, and if that's the case, it's a waste of time and a pain in the ass because there are thousands of books with white people in them and they're not all the same."

Smith's objection is a politicized one: that writers of "ethnic origin" are expected to be representative and hence are marketed and assessed through their origins and the color of their characters' skin, whereas, as she has put it elsewhere:

"Do you go to Don DeLillo and say, 'He doesn't represent middle-class white people enough'? [. . .] No. You give him complete freedom. Why would you limit writers of any ethnicity or gender to be a sex or class politician and give freedom to white writers to write about absolutely anybody?"

What Smith is objecting to is a school of criticism that narrows the options available to non-white writers by insisting on reading their work through the lens of ethnicity. Such readings not only racialize interpretation, but also operate a double standard, as "middle-class white people" are not submitted to the same interpretive expectations. Smith exposes the hypocrisy of the literary establishment, and also the manner in which marketing frequently works through suspect analogies. However, in the desire to right such critical wrongs, and also, it might be suspected, as a young writer keen to assert her own literary identity, Smith is too quick to deny her connection to Rushdie and Kureishi, and the fruitful comparative readings that could be made of their work.

The theme of British immigrant life is not the only fictional motif Smith shares with Kureishi. Similarities of technique and tone also unite them. On its publication, Kureishi's *The Buddha of Suburbia* was widely praised for its energetic and humorous treatment of multiculturalism through the characters of Karim, his family and friends. "My name is Karim Amir," the novel opens, "and I am an Englishman born and bred, almost. I am often considered to be a funny kind of Englishman, a new breed as it were, having emerged from two old histories. But I don't care — Englishman I am (though not proud of it), from the South London suburbs and going somewhere." A generous tone with satirical intent typifies the narratives of both *The Buddha of Suburbia* and *White Teeth*, and the function of Kureishi and Smith's comedy is simultaneously to provoke and to entertain.

Other influences upon *White Teeth* range from the aforementioned Martin Amis and Charles Dickens to the Laurence Sterne of *The Life and Opinions of Tristram Shandy, Gentleman* (1759–67). Smith has admitted how her extensive reading spills into her writing, self-effacingly calling *White Teeth* "'a huge-scale rip-off of many other writers,'" including Kingsley Amis, Philip Larkin, Charles Dickens, E M Forster, Jeneatte Winterson, Julian Barnes, and Martin Amis. She has also professed herself a fan of George Eliot, Vladimir Nabokov, Thomas Pynchon, and Raymond Carver. While Smith's critics may not be as damning as she is of herself, these, and further, influences have been identified by the reviews of her work. Such intertextual largesse, and its implications for the ways in which the novel can be read, suggest that the question of influence is also a debate about the nature of interpretation, the manner in which new writing is defined, and the cultural and political consequences of both acts. In *White Teeth*, Smith proves herself to be in combative mood with regard to these debates, teasingly placing "a little featureless squib called Mart, Jules, Ian" in a Willesden school playground (p. 291). A glancing reference, it would seem, to the middle-aged, middle-class and white triumvirate of English letters: Martin Amis, Julian Barnes, and Ian McEwan.

Following the publication of *White Teeth*, Smith has published a variety of material, including further short stories, journalism, and her introduction to Lewis Carroll, and edited a collection of erotica by young writers, *Piece of Flesh* (2001). She has also been writer-in-residence at the Institute of Contemporary Arts in London. For her next full-length work, she plans to publish a novel entitled *The Autograph Man*, featuring an obsessive half-Jewish, half-Chinese autograph collector as protagonist, and will deal with mystical religion, pornography, and the nature of fame. This last topic is one that must lie close to Smith's heart: celebrity and exhaustive critical attention have been attendant on her literary career from its beginning, and there are now heavy expectations on a new book from this young writer. What that book will be like, and how it will be received by the critics and readers, is yet to be decided, but the evidence of *White Teeth* would suggest that Smith's future writing career will be worth following with great scrutiny.

2

The Novel

f

Introduction

White Teeth is a complex work, featuring multiple locations, time frames and characters. It is also a lengthy novel, extending to over 500 pages in the paperback edition. This chapter offers an introduction to—and interpretation of—the places, periods, and people of *White Teeth*. It divides into two main sections, "Themes" and "Style." The Themes are further divided into the subsections "Multiculturalism," "History," "Generations and Gender," and "Chance, Choice, and Fate;" Style into subsections discussing "Narrative and the Narrator," "Voice," and "Genre." Each of these subsections explores different aspects of the novel, although the intersections of plot, characterization and language mean they also reflect on one another. Page references are to the Penguin edition.

Themes

MULTICULTURALISM

Approximately halfway through *White Teeth*, shortly after the introduction of the Chalfens to the story, the narrator steps in to comment upon the proceedings. Irie and Millat, having been caught
smoking a joint with Joshua Chalfen, are given by their liberal
headmaster the discipline of going to the Chalfen household to
study. Joyce Chalfen, the mother of the family, is delighted with
this development, and expresses her pleasure by claiming that her
youngest son finds strangers—"'especially brown strangers'"—"'really stimulating'" (p. 326). The satirical portrait of the Chalfens
then pauses, as the narrator launches into a disquisition upon immigrancy and multiculturalism inspired by Joyce's words:

This has been the century of strangers, brown, yellow and white. This has
been the century of the great immigrant experiment. It is only this late in
the day that you can walk into a playground and find Isaac Leung by the
fish pond, Danny Rahman in the football cage, Quang O'Rourke bouncing
a basketball, and Irie Jones humming a tune. Children with first and last
names on a direct collision course. Names that secrete within them mass
exodus, cramped boats and planes, cold arrivals, medical checks. (p. 326)

Here, in a London playground, are children—including one of the
novel's protagonists—whose ethnic identities have become con-
fused as a result of hybridization. This mixed-up situation is one of
the abiding themes of *White Teeth*, a theme that incorporates the
legacy of empire, the assemblage of immigrants in the old imperial
centers, and the multicultural societies that are thus produced.

The cast of *White Teeth* echoes the multiculturalism of the playground. The plot revolves around three main families — the British and Jamaican Joneses, the Bangladeshi Iqbals, and the Jewish Catholic Chalfens — over the course of several generations. All the families live in Willesden, and are connected through the youngest generation, who attend the same schools. The links between the families go further back, though, as Archie Jones and Samad Iqbal first meet on active service in World War II. This unlikely friendship is the linchpin of the novel, and its trajectory from mid- to late-twentieth century encompasses much of the historical sweep of *White Teeth*. To introduce the themes of *White Teeth*, then, is to be introduced to its characters, beginning with the Joneses.

THE JONESES

Archie Jones is of undistinguished background, as he is ready to admit when he first meets Samad, but is of "'Good honest English stock'" (p. 99). Such an epithet defines Archie's uncomplicated and pragmatic approach to life, though his incapacity to make decisions without the toss of a coin is a characteristic all of his own. Archie is an unimportant man:

a man whose significance in the Greater Scheme of Things could be figured along familiar ratios:

Pebble: Beach.
Raindrop: Ocean.
Needle: Haystack. (p. 11)

Brought up in Brighton, he joins up in the final year of the war at the age of 17, managing to convince the army that he is old enough to be admitted. Thus far, his horizons have been severely limited, and so when he is assigned to a tank which is also occupied by Samad, all the white boy can do is stare at his new comrade-in-arms, who is "the warm colour of baked bread" (p. 83). Yet despite such inauspicious beginnings, a friendship develops, although after the end of the war they are not reunited until the 1970s.

On his way home from the war, Archie meets and marries an Italian waitress, Ophelia. Their marriage is predestined to fail, though, because of Archie's incapacity to love women unless surmounted by "haloes" (p. 8) and Ophelia's family tree of madmen and hysterics. The marriage quickly deteriorates, yet takes thirty years to break up completely. In the meantime, Archie's attempts to become a war correspondent are rebutted by a snooty man who points out his lack of experience ("*War experience isn't really relevant*" (p. 14), as he puts it). Instead he settles for a job in, as Archie writes on his second marriage certificate, "Advertising: (Printed Leaflets)" (p. 50). His second wife Clara's more comical dismissal is that he "'. . . folds paper for a living, dear *Jesus*'" (p. 82).

The one moment of glory in his humdrum life ("A dull childhood, a bad marriage, a dead-end job" (p. 14) as his pre-suicide flashback reveals to him) is a joint thirteenth place in track cycling in the 1948 London Olympics, an event which he receives reminders of in the strange form of letters from the Swedish Horst Ibelgaufts, with whom he shared the place. Yet by the end of 1974, deserted by the wife he didn't love, Archie is ready to commit suicide, although he cannot make the decision without tossing a coin. Chance decrees he will kill himself, and so early on New Year's Day 1975, he parks his car in Cricklewood Broadway, feeds a Hoover pipe from the exhaust to the window, and waits to die.

His "second [. . .] chance" (p. 4) comes in the shape of the irascible halal butcher, Mo Hussein-Ishmael, in whose delivery area Archie has parked. Mo insists that Archie move on, his property "'not licensed'" for suicides (p. 7). Granted this "second chance,"

Archie drives round London, goes to an "End of the World" party
(p. 20), and meets the nineteen-year-old Clara, to whom he is married in six weeks.

Clara's entrance into *White Teeth*, and Archie's life, is a dramatic
descent in a red halter neck and tight yellow flares down the stair-
case into Archie's arms. She has "possibly [only] one imperfection
[. . .] A complete lack of teeth in the top of her mouth" (p. 24).
Clara Jones, née Bowden, is Jamaican. She arrives as an immigrant
in 1972 with her mother Hortense, who is "enraged" at waiting for
her lethargic husband Darcus, an earlier arrival, to arrange their
passage to England. Instead, she decides to "make the journey on
her own steam," prompting the narrator's comment that "Steam was
something Hortense had in abundance" (p. 31). Hortense is one in
a series of emphatic female figures in the Bowden family tree,
which, for all its uncertainties, has a strong matrilineal structure;
"Russian dolls," going back one inside the other (p. 356). Hortense's
mother, Ambrosia, gave birth to her daughter during the Kingston
earthquake of 1907, the father the English colonist Captain Charlie
"Whitey" Durham. Irie, Clara's daughter by Archie, thus is de-
scended from a black maternal line and a partially white paternal
line, begun in the colonial era and continued in postcolonial London.

Hortense and Clara join Darcus in his dingy basement flat.
Hortense is a Jehovah's Witness, and Clara is sent into St. Jude's,
her predominantly Irish Catholic school, with a satchel full of
copies of the *Watchtower*, a task that as "a six-foot black missionary
in knee socks" equals "social leprosy" (p. 29). While knocking on
doors in Lambeth, though, she comes across Ryan Topps, another
school misfit and the object of her affections. They start going out,
but while Ryan introduces Clara to scooter rides, weed, and the
north London squat where she will meet Archie, Hortense converts

Ryan to her religion. This betrayal leads Clara to lose her teeth in a scooter accident, and to provide the theme for the New Year's party Archie stumbles into. Hortense and Ryan stay at home waiting for the end of the world their religion has prophesied. The melancholy of losing her religion pushes Clara into the unlikely arms of Archie, and a "peculiar" marriage (p. 3).

After her marriage, Clara's character very much takes second place to her supporting role as wife and mother. Irie, however, becomes a central character in the latter stages of the novel. Unhappy about her physical appearance and suffering unrequited love, her teenage angst is also influenced by genealogy. She has the body shape of her Jamaican forebears, and hair she fantasizes of changing into "Straight straight long black sleek flickable tossable shakeable touchable finger-through-able wind-blowable hair. With a fringe" (p. 273). These physical characteristics render Irie "A stranger in a stranger land" (p. 266), the focus of multicultural alienation. Her disastrous attempts to change her hair in a Willesden salon provide one of the highlights of *White Teeth*, a scene of sharply observed comedy and feeling for the beleaguered adolescent. It is through the character of Irie that the anxieties of youth and immigrant communities are displayed, and her function in the novel is often to articulate opinions that the narrative voice can only do more intrusively. Irie's splenetic outburst on the bus at the end of the novel, precipitated by the squabbling of the Jones and Iqbal clans, is a prime example. She contrasts them with other families:

"What a peaceful existence. What a *joy* their lives must be. They open a door and all they've got behind it is a bathroom or a lounge. Just neutral spaces. And not this endless maze of present rooms and past rooms and the things said in them years ago and everybody's old historical shit all over the place. They're not constantly making the same old mistakes. They're not always hearing the same old shit. [. . .] And every single fucking day is not this huge battle between who they are and who they should be, what they were and what they will be. Go on, ask them. And they'll tell you. No mosque. Maybe a little church. Hardly any sin. Plenty of forgiveness. No attics. No shit in attics. No skeletons in cupboards. No great-grandfathers. I will put twenty quid down *now* that Samad is the only person in here who knows the inside bloody leg measurement of his great-grandfather. And you know *why* they don't know? Because *it doesn't fucking matter*. As far as they're concerned, it's the *past*." (pp. 514–5)

Irie's outburst, its rage against history, destiny and the bonds of family, is prompted by her own situation. Her dislike of her physical appearance is fueled by her unrequited love for one of the twins, Millat, but she has sex with both twins within half an hour. The resulting pregnancy leaves her caught in a genetic trap, unable to distinguish who the father is. This double parentage *may* make the "fatherless little girl [. . .] a puppet clipped of paternal strings" (p. 541), but the narrator will do no more than speculate. The narrator also foretells at the end of the novel that Irie and Joshua become lovers as "you can only avoid your fate for so long." The conditional tense of these speculations promises not a "future[. . .] perfect," but a future that may well be as fraught with the traps of history, family and destiny as the "past [. . .] tense" (p. 541).

Irie jumps at the chance to act as an informal PA for Marcus Chalfen, though she is later displaced by Magid. Her contact with the Chalfen family is a revelation of a class-based nature, a world of middle-class intellectuals with whom "she *wanted* to merge [. . .] to be of one flesh; separated from the chaotic, random flesh of her own family and transgenically fused with another" (p. 342). Her own decision about her future, made as a consequence of an off-hand remark in a letter to Magid by Marcus, is to become a dentist, tying her to the novel's structure of metaphor. Whether this decision is accomplished is not revealed.

THE IQBALS

Samad, a Bangladeshi Muslim, recently married to his long-promised, much younger wife, Alsana Begum, arrives in England in the spring of 1973. They move first to the east end of London, but wary of racist violence, and eager to rekindle the war-time friendship between himself and Archie, Samad moves to Willesden. Despite being university-educated in Delhi, Samad has problems finding work in London, and is reduced to working as a deferential waiter in the Palace, a restaurant owned by a distant cousin. Samad dreams of asserting his humanity by wearing a placard that reveals his personal history:

I AM NOT A WAITER. I HAVE BEEN A STUDENT, A SCIENTIST, A SOLDIER, MY WIFE IS CALLED ALSANA, WE LIVE IN EAST LONDON BUT WE WOULD LIKE TO MOVE NORTH. I AM A MUSLIM BUT ALLAH HAS FORSAKEN ME OR I HAVE FORSAKEN ALLAH, I'M NOT SURE. I HAVE A FRIEND—ARCHIE—AND OTHERS. I AM FORTY-NINE BUT WOMEN STILL TURN IN THE STREET. SOMETIMES. (P. 58)

Samad's imaginary placard is symptomatic of the portrayal of character in *White Teeth*: at once deeply empathetic for the lot of the frustrated waiter while, through the stroke of comic timing of the final word, deflating his pretensions. Samad's troubled relationship with his god preempts the development of his character in the plot, as he fears for Allah, morality, and cultural tradition. In a crisis meeting with Archie in O'Connell's, he expounds these fears through his observation of his sisters-in-law's children:

"all their children are nothing but trouble. They won't go to mosque, they don't pray, they speak strangely, they dress strangely, they eat all kinds of rubbish, they have intercourse with God knows who. No respect for tradition. People call it assimilation when it is nothing but corruption. Corruption!" (p. 190)

His anxiety about the impact living in England has on the second generation is equally pertinent to his own situation. Samad swings between the poles of faith and secularism, between absolutism and compromise, between rejecting and falling prey to temptation. His tussles with Allah and his conscience are represented by two maxims: *"To the pure all things are pure"* and *"Can't say fairer than that"* (p. 137). The former is an attempt to justify his unholy activities of masturbation, food, drink, and his desire for Poppy Burt-Jones, his children's music teacher, the latter a plea for fairness and understanding, a process of "deal"-making with Allah (p. 139). Yet such deals, even his "New Deal" (p. 140), cannot salve his conscience when he begins an affair with Poppy. Samad decides that he is faced with "a choice of *morality*": he is an unsuitable father and needs to concentrate on "'saving my sons'" (p. 189). The decision he comes to is to send one (he can't afford both) of his sons back to Bangladesh to be educated in the proper tradition.

Alsana's reaction to the decision he makes without even consulting her is to begin a war of attrition, by determining "never to say *yes* to him, never to say *no* to him," to answer his every question with a variation of "'maybe, Samad Miah, maybe not'" (p. 213). Her *"exquisite* revenge" (p. 214) for the uncertainty Samad has placed her in about Magid's welfare is a form of passive resistance, one manifestation of trouble between the genders in *White Teeth.* Alsana is not the submissive wife that either Samad or the patronizing liberal feminists "with the piteous, saddened smiles they reserved for subjugated Muslim women" of the novel expect her to be (p. 131). Alsana may initially be "a breath of fresh air" to the newly married, rejuvenated Samad, but her "shrewd eyes" suggest that she is unlikely to conform to expectation (p. 12). Her sharp wit confirms this suggestion. Her most caustic remarks are reserved for Samad and Archie, but her satirical opinions on arranged marriages, the Chalfens, French cinema, and false notions of authenticity are as picturesque. Alsana is aware of the hypocrisies of both west and east, of secularism and religion, and as such provides a voice of comic reason in *White Teeth*. Her analysis of racial origins, after perusing the *Reader's Digest Encyclopedia*, is that "'It just goes to show [. . .] you go back and back and back and it's still easier to find the correct Hoover bag than to find one pure person, one pure faith, on the globe. Do you think anybody is English? Really English? It's a fairy-tale!'" (p. 236).

Alsana, although from a wealthy Bengali family, also finds herself forced into hard work in England:

banging away at the old Singer that sat in the kitchen, sewing together pieces of black plastic for a shop called Domination in Soho (many were the nights Alsana would hold up a piece of clothing she had just made, following the pattern she was given, and wonder what on earth it was). (p. 55)

This vignette demonstrates Smith's witty ability to encapsulate her characters' lives, though there is also a nagging doubt that the description is more successful as comic effect than as rounded characterization.

Alsana's relationship with Samad, before it enters its phase of passive resistance, has a more explosive nature. Domestic violence occurs in slapstick style:

Second round. Samad slapped Alsana. Alsana right hooked him in the stomach and then followed up with a blow to the left cheekbone. She then made a dash to the back door, but Samad caught her by the waist, rugby-tackled her, dragged her down and elbowed her in the coccyx. Alsana, being heavier than Samad, knelt up, lifting him; flipped him over and dragged him out into the garden, where she kicked him twice as he lay on the floor [. . .] (p. 200)

Watching this fight, betting on the result, are Samad and Alsana's twins, Magid (the elder by two minutes) and Millat. Despite being identical, the twins express their separate identities from a young age. Magid is more studious, Millat a star footballer. On the twins' ninth birthday, Samad and Alsana discover, to their dismay, that Magid has been calling himself "Mark Smith" to his white chess-club friends (p. 151). His youthful rejection of his identity presages the later, paradoxical, results of Samad's decision to send him back to Bangladesh.

Millat, who stays in England, becomes the source of anxiety to all concerned with him. *"The Trouble with Millat"* is, to Samad's mind, symptomatic of second-generation corruption. Millat is "[i]n the language of the street [. . .] a rudeboy, a badman, at the forefront, changing image as often as shoes; sweet-as, safe, *wicked*, leading kids up hills to play football, downhill to rifle fruit machines, out of schools, into video shops." (p. 217) As he grows older, the "Pied Piper of Willesden Green" extends his charms to "smitten girls," his "fierce good looks" and "juvenile delinquency" making him "a street boy, a leader of tribes" (p. 218). He styles himself on the Hollywood Mafia heroes he encounters in the video stores, a quite different paternal line from that of Samad: "Godfathers, blood-brothers, pacinodeniros, men in black who looked good, who talked fast, who never waited a (motherfuckin') table, who had two, fully functioning, gun-toting hands" (p. 217). Millat's secular idols and teenage successes, however, do not put him beyond the reach of his religion. In January 1989, he travels with a group of friends to Bradford to take part in protests against a "dirty book" by an unnamed writer, a reference to Salman Rushdie and the controversy caused by the publication of *The Satanic Verses* (p. 233). Back home in Willesden Green, Samad and Alsana see their younger son appear on a TV news report, burning copies of the book. Alsana, enraged by what she perceives as her son's intolerance, sets out to teach him the lesson that "'Either everything is sacred or nothing is'" by burning "[a]ll his secular stuff": records, posters, T-shirts, club fliers, trainers, books, videos, and his guitar (p. 237). This moment represents the beginning of Millat's struggle between faith and secularism.

Millat later becomes involved with a satirically-drawn Islamic fundamentalist youth group, the Keepers of the Eternal and Victo-rious Islamic Nation, or KEVIN ("'We are aware [. . .] that we have an acronym problem,'" admits the solemn Hifan, in another of the memorable comic vignettes of the novel [p. 295]). Millat tries to live as KEVIN prescribes, studying the Qurʾān, and largely giving up smoking, drugs, alcohol, and women. His weakness, though, is in his attempt "To purge oneself of the taint of the West" (p. 444). Even as he styles himself as Islamic, the refrains of his Mafia screen heroes sing in his head, the *GoodFellas* line "As far back as I can remember, I always wanted to be a gangster" rephrased as "As far back as I can remember, I always wanted to be a Muslim" (p. 446). Millat's double vision looks east and west, incorporating religion and the movies, fundamentalism and the teenage badlands of the London streets. He is depicted as "st[anding] schizophrenic, one foot in Bengal and one in Willesden" (p. 219). Despite living many miles apart, he finds his life inexplicably intertwined with that of his twin.

Magid's eventual return from Bangladesh to work on Marcus Chalfen's scientific projects is revealed to Samad as a failing in his personal investigation into the principles of nature and nurture. As he laments to Irie:

"The one I send home comes out a pukka Englishman, white suited, silly wig lawyer. The one I keep here is fully paid-up green bow-tie-wearing fundamentalist terrorist. I sometimes wonder why I bother." (p. 407)

Magid's reappearance in London as the "'pukka Englishman'" is a reversal of the trope of "the returned man" of postcolonial writing, in which colonial subjects are sent abroad for their education and return filled with Western ideas. The apotheosis of Magid's unexpected transition to Western rationalism is his request to be served "'a juicy, yet well-done, tomato ketchup-ed bacon sandwich. On brown'" in O'Connell's (p. 450). Despite Abdul-Mickey's "most hallowed, sacred rule" of "NO PORK," Magid insists on his order, thus representing through the plate of food eventually served to him personally by Abdul-Mickey the defeat of tradition, Muslim values, and his father's experiment (p. 450). Smith's humorous fictional creation of a moment of faith tested and found wanting finds a parallel in Rushdie's work, in the essay "'In God We Trust'" (1985; reprinted in his volume *Imaginary Homelands* [1991]), where he describes how as a fifteen-year-old in an English public school he bought "a rather tasteless ham sandwich, and so partook for the first time of the forbidden flesh of the swine." The dramatization of Magid's consumption of the "forbidden flesh" affords a striking yet comic symbol of the debate set up in *White Teeth* between faith and secularism.

When Magid and Millat are eventually reunited, they find themselves on opposing factions. Magid is working for Marcus on his genetically engineered FutureMouse, while Millat and KEVIN are fervently against what they see as an "'abomination'" to "*The Sanctity of Creation*" (p. 463). Their reunion takes place in a "blank room" (p. 463), but very quickly:

> they cover the room with history—past, present and future history (for there is such a thing)—they take what was blank and smear it with the stinking shit of the past like excitable, excremental children. They cover this neutral room in themselves. Every gripe, the earliest memories, every debated principle, every contested belief. (p. 464)

Sibling rivalry, the transcontinental experiment that Samad plays with their lives, and immigrant legacy divide them, but, at the very end of the novel, their destinies are once more brought together as the police and the courts cannot tell the two sufficiently apart to prosecute Millat for shooting Archie. The confusion of evidence and counter-evidence proves a metaphor for the mess of multicultural experience, and the decisions it makes between assimilation and corruption, fundamentalism and compromise, schizophrenia and hybridity.

THE CHALFENS

The Chalfen family does not occupy such a large proportion of the narrative as the Joneses and Iqbals, but does nonetheless come to play a central part in its development. Marcus and Joyce Chalfen, the parents, are first introduced at a school parent-governor meeting as "an ageing hippy couple both dressed in pseudo-Indian garb" (p. 131) whom Poppy describes as "'such *nice* people — *intellectuals*,'" although she makes the statement "as if it were some exotic disease of the tropics" (p. 132). Joyce, a gardening writer, describes the next generation of her family in her bestselling book of the 1970s, *The New Flower Power*, as "a cross-pollination between a lapsed-Catholic horticulturalist feminist and an intellectual Jew!" (p. 309). Joyce's smug, and spurious, assertion of her children's superiority is a parody of the hybridity for which *White Teeth* has been feted. The satirical tone Smith adopts in the extract from Joyce's book offers, then, a warning to any critic wanting to read her multicultural portrayals as simple celebration. Marcus's pomposity about the possibilities of his science also interrogates the notion that transgenic futures are the most desirable. He quite consciously takes on a God-like role, but neither his science nor his character is portrayed in a favorable light.

As a result of the headmaster's injunction, Millat and Irie go to the Chalfens' home and become caught up in their social and scientific experimentation. Joyce decides that Millat will be her personal crusade, while Irie works for Marcus before being supplanted by Magid. Alsana is particularly resentful of Joyce's attempts to seize Millat from her, and her miscomprehension of the Chalfen surname as "Chaffinches" leads her to see them as "'little scavenging English birds pecking at all the best seeds!'" (p. 344):

"I am saying these people are taking my son away from me! Birds with teeth! They're Englishifying him completely! They're deliberately leading him away from his culture and his family and his religion—" (p. 345)

The Chalfens, although a secular family, nonetheless invent their own creed of "Chalfenism": "They referred to themselves as nouns, verbs and occasionally adjectives: *It's the Chalfen way, And then he came out with a real Chalfenism, He's Chalfening again, We need to be a bit more Chalfenist about this*" (p. 314). The self-satisfaction of the elder Chalfens, and their patronizing attitudes towards Millat, Irie, and their families, make them insufferable. The stereotyping is not tempered with as much empathy as her depictions of the Joneses and Iqbals.

Joshua, the eldest son, becomes disaffected with "Chalfenism." In a direct challenge to his father's profession, he joins a militant animal rights group, FATE, which, like KEVIN, infiltrates the final meeting at the Perret Institute with subversive intent. The tensions that crack the surface of Joyce's vision of her perfect cross-pollinated family are the habitual ones of generational conflict, but are also inflected with the ideological fervor and misgivings of their environment.

An introduction to the Joneses, Iqbals, and Chalfens already indicates the multicultural diversity of *White Teeth*, though other characters, religious groups, and ethnic origins also populate the novel. Archie and Samad's cross-cultural friendship is consolidated in O'Connell's Pool House, their "home from home" (p. 184). O'Connell's is "neither Irish nor a pool house" (p. 183), but "half café, half gambling den" (p. 12) run by the Iraqi Abdul-Mickey (whose pragmatic male family trait of adding an English name to "Abdul" is itself a hybrid tendency). O'Connell's is both a male refuge from wives and children, and also a microcosm of the racially eclectic Willesden Green. It is a place where diversity is accepted in a jocular fashion, and deemed less important than the everyday business of male life.

Yet such comfortable multiculturalism is not the only way contemporary British society is portrayed. The "Samad 1984, 1857" part of the novel is prefaced by the infamous remark made by the Conservative politician Norman Tebbit in 1990, "*'The cricket test— which side do they cheer for?. . . . Are you still looking back to where you came from or where you are?'*" (p. 123). Tebbit's "cricket test" was a rebuke to the British immigrant who refused to assimilate wholeheartedly to British culture. Its reference to cricket both trivialized and encapsulated the issues that Samad himself grapples with. It also sounded a loud warning to any one of the groups of immigrants to Britain who came from countries with—not least because of British colonialism—strong cricketing traditions: the West Indies, India, and Pakistan amongst them. The "cricket test" is an analogy for the fraught issue of the location of a migrant's physical and mental "home."

The issue of home and origins haunts *White Teeth*. The boisterous children, on their way to deliver Harvest Festival bounty to Mr. J. P. Hamilton, are confronted by the racist refrain of their fellow bus passengers:

"Our stop!" cried Magid, shooting to his feet and pulling the bell cord too many times.

"*If you ask me,*" said one disgruntled OAP to another, "*they should all go back to their own . . .*"

But this, the oldest sentence in the world, found itself stifled by the ringing of bells and the stamping of feet, until it retreated under the seats with the chewing gum. (p. 163)

The old people are impotent in the face of Magid, Millat, and Irie's impudent youth, their racist comment stopped in its tracks before the word "country" can be spoken. For as well as a battle between nationalism and multiculturalism, enfolded in this scene is a generational conflict, which is sustained when the children arrive at their destination. Mr. J. P. Hamilton, surprised by "three dark-skinned children" (p. 168) at his door, eventually lets them into his house, but launches into a tale of his experience of killing "'nigger[s]'" in the Congo by the light reflected by the "'flash of white'" from their teeth (pp.171, 2). He rubbishes the idea that the twins' father could have served in the British Army. The children run away while the old man's reminiscences and exhortations to brush their teeth run on, escaping his incipient racism.

Even supposedly liberal characters in the book exert themselves over the children's difference. Joyce expresses her delight at having "'exotic,'" "'brown strangers'" in the house, and insists on knowing where they are from "'*originally*,'" a question that Millat deflates with his response of "'Whitechapel'" (p. 319) — not the subcontinental reply she was expecting. In *White Teeth*, racism or insistence on ethnic difference is frequently met with such comic deflation. The novel's form of resistance is not overtly political, but comedic and tactical, showing racism as out-of-date. Alsana's typically off-the-wall metaphor of racial origins and Hoover bags is symptomatic of Smith's approach.

The theme of the immigrant's attitude to home is also addressed in a characteristically cheerful manner, though Samad's consideration of dislocation and belonging is one occasion where melancholy cuts through the humor:

"But you have made a devil's pact . . . it drags you in and suddenly you are unsuitable to return, your children are unrecognizable, you belong nowhere."

"Oh, that's not true, surely."

"And then you begin to give up the *very idea* of belonging. Suddenly this thing, this *belonging*, it seems like some long, dirty lie . . . and I begin to believe that birthplaces are accidents, that everything is an *accident*. But if you believe that, where do you go? What do you do? What does anything matter?" (p. 407)

Samad's anxieties and Alsana's fears that Millat is being taken away from her by the Chalfens, or will marry a white girl, are confirmed by the narrator, who compares the mind-set of the racist and the immigrant:

it makes an immigrant laugh to hear the fears of the nationalist, scared of infection, penetration, miscegenation, when this is small fry, *peanuts*, compared to what the immigrant fears — dissolution, *disappearance*. (p. 327)

Racism, though often deflected by the characters and the narrator, still makes its presence felt in *White Teeth*. Archie comes face to face with it in his boss's attitude to Clara. It is racism that propels Millat to protest against *The Satanic Verses* (pp. 233–4), racism that persuades Mo, the butcher who saves Archie's life, to join KEVIN (pp. 472–3), and racism that precipitates the Iqbal family's move from the east end to Willesden, as Alsana reflects:

Willesden was not as pretty as Queens Park, but it was a nice area. No denying it. Not like Whitechapel, where that madman E-knock someoneoranother gave a speech that forced them into the basement while kids broke the windows with their steel-capped boots. Rivers of blood silly-billy nonsense. (pp. 62–3)

For Alsana's family, the incendiary rhetoric of the right-wing politician Enoch Powell's 1968 "rivers of blood" speech has a very real impact. Nonetheless, Alsana's distinctive voice reinterprets the violence, and while racism is ever present in *White Teeth*, it is continually greeted with comic derision rather than fearful submission. Smith refuses to preach an anti-racist message in *White Teeth*, preferring instead to turn prejudice into a "nonsense." It might be argued that this betrays a lack of political commitment on Smith's part, but the insistent representation of racism as an absurdity has its own politics. A more salient criticism might be that her representative mode is too optimistic.

Alsana is thankful to have moved from Whitechapel, even if her feelings towards Willesden are not completely positive. Any claims for the liberality of her new borough are dismissed as "'Liberal? Hosh-kosh nonsense!'" (p. 63). Yet in the reviews of *White Teeth*, Smith's Willesden is repeatedly taken as a positive representation of the energies of the melting pot. Certainly, the headmistress of the children's junior school details with pride the school's wideranging multicultural calendar:

"As I am sure you are aware, the school already recognizes a great variety of religious and secular events: amongst them, Christmas, Ramadan, Chinese New Year, Diwali, Yom Kippur, Hanukkah, the birthday of Haile Selassie, and the death of Martin Luther King. The Harvest Festival is part of the school's ongoing commitment to religious diversity, Mr Iqbal." (p. 129)

The school's vision of racial and religious diversity is neither accepted by Samad (who thinks the Harvest Festival a "'pagan'" event that should be removed from the curriculum [p. 129]) or treated unsatirically. Poppy wants to support Samad's plea for more Muslim events to be incorporated into the school calendar, but does so on the grounds that they "'would be so much more . . . colourful'" (p. 133). Smith's inscription of Poppy's wish to add local colour to the school, tying the events in "'with art work, music'" (p. 133), provides an implicit critique of how many critics would respond to *White Teeth*, applauding it for representing the brightly varied environment of Willesden Green. Smith may represent an optimistic view of multiculturalism in *White Teeth*, but she does not do so without also satirizing the liberal platitudes that would inform her own reception.

Reading *White Teeth* as a postcolonial novel, and Zadie Smith as an "ethnically interesting" author, is to risk turning multiculturalism into an aesthetic commodity. Graham Huggan's work *The Postcolonial Exotic: Marketing the Margins* (2001), provides an informative framework from which to view Smith's postcolonial representations and her internal critique, apparent in passages such as Poppy's breathless appreciation of "'Indian culture'" (p. 133) — and also, to introduce a sexualized element — her physical appreciation of Samad as an "'Omar Sharif'" look-a-like (p. 136). Huggan's notion of "exoticism," developed through the writings of numerous theorists, is of "a particular mode of aesthetic *perception* — one which renders people, objects and places strange even as it domesticates them, and which effectively manufactures otherness even as it claims to surrender to its immanent mystery." The play *White Teeth* makes with otherness and familiarity, representing the simultaneously strange and domestic, suggests that reading the novel alongside the questions posed by Huggan would be a productive undertaking. Huggan debates what the implications are once (as with the overwhelming success of *White Teeth*) cultural marginality becomes central:

If exoticism has *arrived* in the "centre," it still *derives* from the cultural margins or, perhaps more accurately, from a commodified discourse of cultural marginality. How is value ascribed to, and regulated within, the cultural margins? What is the role of exoticism in putatively marginal modes of production and representation? What happens when marginal products, explicitly valued for their properties of "resistance," are seconded to the mainstream as a means of reinvigorating mainstream culture?

Huggan goes on to investigate the "staged marginalities" of writers such as Rushdie, Hanif Kureishi, and V S Naipaul. Considering Smith from a similar theoretical perspective reveals how her ironic inscriptions of the reception of postcolonial cultures can be understood as a paradoxical strategy of both acceptance and resistance, an argument for both her critical and commercial success, and for the novel's endurance beyond the simple excitement provoked by its multicultural theme.

As has been discussed in the previous chapter, Smith has expressed her exasperation at the continual comparisons made by critics between *White Teeth* and the writing of Rushdie and Kureishi. Indeed, only reductive readings will transpire from turning the critique of *White Teeth* into a simple hunt for literary influence. There are, though, similarities of characterization worth noting between *White Teeth* and Kureishi's *The Black Album*, for example, in which the protagonist's brother styles himself, as does Millat, on Mafia movies: "Time and again he watched *Once upon a Time in America, Scarface,* and *The Godfather* — as careers documentaries." Kureishi also writes, in a parallel to the boredom expressed by the wives and children whenever Samad and Archie talk about the war, that Shahid's mother refuses to humor her husband by "listening to his accounts of the war." The Islamic "posse" of *The Black Album* pushes the secular Shahid to consider casting off his smoking, drinking, and womanizing habits. KEVIN's effect on Millat is similar.

Such intertextual links, and the "'[s]erious goings on in Bradford'" (p. 236) of *The Satanic Verses* affair, make reading *White Teeth* alongside Rushdie and Kureishi a legitimate enterprise, though the questions posed by Huggan, and the extent to which different versions of the "exotic" are conflated without proper analysis, should be constantly foregrounded. *White Teeth* is a postcolonial fiction, it speaks of race and multiculturalism and it is more than appropriate to discuss it in such terms. Nonetheless, to do so as an uncritical celebration of the bright multicultural color of the Willesden streets, is as critically naïve an interpretive act as viewing the novel as a product of (in Huggan's phrase) "the spiralling commodification of cultural difference" would be a cynical one. To read *White Teeth* with neither naïveté nor cynicism will be the chief challenge to future critics of Smith's work.

History

When Magid and Millat are reunited after years of separation, their meeting is crowded with their "past, present and future history." At this point the narrator quite literally pauses the action to consider Zeno's paradoxes as metaphors for how the twins, and immigrants in general, cannot escape these histories:

The harder Achilles tries to catch the tortoise, the more eloquently the tortoise expresses its advantage. Likewise, the brothers will race towards the future only to find they more and more eloquently express their past, that place where they have *just been*. Because this is the other thing about immigrants ('fugees, émigrés, travellers): they cannot escape their history any more than you yourself can lose your shadow. (p. 466)

The inescapability of history is also mentioned a few paragraphs earlier in the rhetoric of the "greenandpleasantlibertarianlandofthefree," into which immigrants step, "[w]e have been told [...] as *blank people*, free of any kind of baggage, happy and willing to leave their difference at the docks." The narrator is skeptical of the vision of "Mr Schmutters and Mr Banajii [...] merrily [...] weaving their way through Happy Multicultural Land" proffered by the anonymous authority of the passive tense (p. 465). The compound noun and capitalization also flag the satirical intent. For Magid and Millat, for all immigrants, such a vision is a fantasy, and if the creation of "Happy Multicultural Land" is contingent upon immigrants becoming *"blank people"* it will never be achieved. If the postcolonial era results in the multicultural diaspora of the metropolitan city, as Homi Bhabha posits, the "post" in "postcolonial" must mean "as a result of and including" rather than simply "afterwards", or even "in opposition to."

This narrative assertion is linked to the novel's epigraph, "What's past is prologue." History and the past are formative and inescapable for the novel's characters. Irie's outburst on the bus expresses her extreme frustration at the knowledge that she cannot evade the burden of history. Samad's consideration of dislocation and belonging contains within it an emphasis on the importance of history to the immigrant, of not becoming disconnected from the past through the act of physical relocation. To Samad, this disconnection — "the land of accidents" — is a "dystopia." Inhabiting a dystopia is frequently the lot of the migrant in Rushdie's fiction: at the beginning of *The Satanic Verses*, for example, the general process of migrancy and the specific event of immigrancy to Britain is violently described as "the debris of the soul, broken memories, sloughed-off selves, severed mother-tongues, violated privacies, untranslatable jokes, extinguished futures, lost loves, the forgotten meaning of hollow, booming words, *land, belonging, home*." Again, to read Smith alongside Rushdie's oeuvre is informative, and Smith's interrogation of the repeated mantra "past tense, future perfect" reveals that her narrative is as pessimistic about "Happy Multicultural Land" as Rushdie's is, and that attitudes of grief, melancholy and despair are as prevalent in her narrative as those of optimism, joy, and reconciliation.

The reader of *White Teeth* will find no easier escape from history than its characters, as references to the past, to origins, and to roots permeate every chapter of the novel. It is present in narrative disquisitions such as the one following Magid and Millat's reconciliation, but also in the novel's structuration of character and plot. The "teeth" of the novel's title become the prevailing metaphor for the novel's historical method, with the three chapters of "root canals" detailing the back histories of Archie, Samad, Mangal Pande, and Hortense Bowden. The first of these tells of Archie and Samad's war-time experience, as the narrator first asks, then answers the question, "how far back do you want? How far will *do*?," taking the reader, "Back, back, *back*. Well, all right, then. Back to Archie spit-clean, pink-faced and polished" (p. 83). The "root canals" depict the origins of Archie and Samad's friendship, but also contains within it the lie on which it was built: that Archie killed "Dr. Sick," the sinister, ailing Nazi scientist captured in a house near the Bulgarian village in which they are waiting for the war to end. Archie, as the narrative eventually reveals, has done no such thing, but his lie is sustained until Dr. Perret's reappearance in his eponymous Institute. History's return unites all the characters at the end of 1992, and propels them — and the rebel FutureMouse, accidentally freed from its glass box — into the possibilities of the future.

Hovering outside the doors of the Perret Institute with her fellow Jehovah's Witnesses is Hortense Bowden. For them, it is an opportunity to spread the word of their apocalyptic message. Hortense was herself born during an event of apocalyptic proportions: the Jamaican earthquake. Her "root canals" describe the matrilineal line leading to Irie, but also the impact of colonization on the Bowden family in the particular form of Captain Charlie Durham.

Contemplating the scantily documented family histories of the Bowden and Jones families against the "elaborate illustrated oak" of the
Chalfens (p. 337), Irie tells Marcus that, "'I guess my family's more
of an oral tradition'" (p. 339). The Bowden family tree is subject to
"rumour, folk-tale and myth" (p. 338), as its intrusion into a scene
in Marcus's study asserts. In the juxtaposition of "Chalfenism versus
Bowdenism," as a chapter heading has it, there is not just a clash of
ideologies, but also a concern with different ways of telling history
and of determining truth.

Such historiographical concerns also plague Samad in his campaign to restore his great-grandfather Mangal Pande to the central
place he thinks he deserves in Indian history. The argument over
this "much neglected, 100-year-old, mildewed yarn" (p. 99) consti-
tutes Pande's "root canals" chapter, in which Samad aligns himself
against his family, friends and "British scholarship from 1857 to the
present day" in defense of his maligned and forgotten antecedent
(p. 250). Over the years Samad and Archie confront each other with
their different "version[s] of events" (p. 255). Samad, summoned by
a nephew to Cambridge University to view what the latter considers,
but does not, for love of his uncle, denounce as "an inferior, insig-
nificant, forgotten piece of scholarship" (p. 258), finds a solitary ally
for his cause. Textual interventions such as the historians' accounts
of Pande, the chart of the "two camps" of opinion (p. 250), and
the timeline for *"The Post-War Reconstruction and Growth of
O'Connell's Pool House"* (pp. 245–7) play with documentary style,
while an awareness of different fashions of telling history are also
incorporated into the chapter. Despite Archie's love of O'Connell's
for its constancy ("Everything was remembered, nothing was lost.
History was never revised or reinterpreted, adapted or whitewashed.
It was as solid and as simple as the encrusted egg on the clock."
[p. 192]), it becomes the site of historical relativity. *White Teeth*,
then, is concerned with history as a motivating force and as a

contestable value, and uses teeth as a narrative device and historio-graphical metaphor.

Historical events also occur in *White Teeth* as a backdrop against which daily lives unfold. Millat becomes embroiled in *The Satanic Verses* affair, but the death of Indira Gandhi and the fall of the Berlin Wall, though commented upon by the characters, do not directly affect them. The hurricane of 1987 has a more direct impact, as the Iqbals and Joneses cower from its force, while Archie attempts to shore up the house with DIY. What these 1980s happenings suggest, though, is that a period can be described not only through its key events, but also through the evocation of day-to-day activity. Talking about the research she undertook for *White Teeth*, Smith mentioned in interview that personal testimonies don't always produce information about the big events of the period, but give anecdotal detail. She refers in this context to a woman who "was born in 1902 [. . .] a ninety-eight [year] old intelligent Jewish lady who's lived this whole century. Ask her what the first World War was like, and she'll tell you the woman she lived next door to in 1916 really knew how to cook rabbit." Such detail, though potentially frustrating to the researcher, can contribute to the creation of atmosphere and characterization in a historical novel. History, then, becomes a foil to the characters, so Indira Gandhi's assassination precipitates another fight between Samad and Alsana about their children. Equally, the fall of the Berlin Wall, *"an historic occasion"* as the narrator slyly puts it (p. 237), prompts an argument between the generations about how the world should be understood.

Generations and Gender

Irie, listening to Samad's anxieties about the lot of the immigrant, thinks that his "dystopi[c]" vision sounds "like *paradise* to her. Sounded like freedom" (p. 408). Irie is desperate to escape history, and Samad's "land of accidents" seems like the "blank room" where a new beginning could be made. Torn between looking forwards and looking back, she tries, in the creation of her own next generation, to begin afresh. Magid, though, thinks she is inextricably bound to history, that for her — as for Magid and Millat — there can be no tabula rasa, as he explains after sleeping with her:

"It seems to me," said Magid finally, as the moon became clearer than the sun, "that you have tried to love a man as if he were an island and you were shipwrecked and you could mark the land with an X. It seems to me it is too late in the day for all that." (p. 463)

Magid's lexicon, with its reference to the dream of the shipwrecked man, contests both Irie's desire to exist beyond the reach of history and the myth of an empty land ripe for colonization. He perfectly encapsulates their quandary as second-generation immigrants. "[T]he great ocean-crossing experiment" does, however, differentiate between its generations, as Samad and his relatives are all too aware, as they ponder *"The Trouble with Millat"* and ask themselves:

what was wrong with all the children [. . .] ? Didn't they have everything they could want? Was there not a substantial garden area, regular meals, clean clothes from Marks 'n' Sparks, A-class top-notch education? Hadn't the elders done their best? Hadn't they all come to this island for a reason? To be safe. Weren't they *safe?* (pp. 218–9)

The handwringing continues, and Samad prematurely congratulates himself for deciding to send Magid back to Bangladesh. The impact of immigration on the families is to drive a wedge between the generations, or, as the narrator has it, "A distance was establishing itself, not simply between *fathersons, oldyoung, bornthererebornhere,* but between those who stayed indoors and those who ran riot outside" (p. 219). Yet this "distance," although foregrounded by the themes of postcolonialism, is also symptomatic of a more general split between the generations. Samad and Archie's friendship is founded on their war experience, but for their young wives and children, it induces a boredom they respond to with "feigned narcolepsy" (p. 225). Their response is not unique: as Archie reviews his life before attempting suicide, he knows that its most important event is a source of indifference to others:

If someone said to Archie, *What have you done in life, then*, or *What's your biggest memory*, well, God help him if he mentioned the war; eyes glazed over, fingers tapped, everybody offered to buy the next round. No one really wanted to *know*. (p. 14)

Even the appreciative Poppy Burt-Jones is wrongfooted by Samad's mention of "the war," a term as old-fashioned to her as "wireless or pianola or water-closet," thinking he must mean the 1982 Falklands conflict (pp. 135, 6). O'Connell's offers a refuge from this disinterest and misunderstanding, a place where the men can relive their experience through the medium of "beer mugs and salt-cellars to represent long-dead people and far-off places" (p. 252). During the two families' discussion of the fall of the Berlin Wall, Archie blunders his way through a claim for the attributes of age, but is halted in his tracks by Alsana's invective:

Archie struggled to continue. "But you can't beat experience, can you? I mean, you two, you're young women still, in a way. Whereas *we*, I mean, we are, like, *wells of experience* the children can use, you know, when they feel the need. We're like encyclopedias. You just can't offer them what we can. In all fairness."

Alsana put her palm on Archie's forehead and stroked it lightly. "You *fool*. Don't you know you're left behind like carriage and horses, like candlewax? Don't you know to them you're old and smelly like yesterday's fishnchip paper? I'll be agreeing with your daughter on one matter of importance [. . .] You two gentlemen talk a great deal of the youknow-what." (p. 242)

Irie's interrupted profanity ("'You two talk such a load of sh-'" [p. 240]), Alsana's colorful imagery, Poppy's miscomprehension, and the glazed eyes of Archie's auditors, all signal the distance between Archie, Samad and their families. Irie's wish to "merge" with the Chalfens is at least in part spurred by her observation of the very different way they carry out intergenerational relationships:

No one in the Jones household [. . .] let speech flow freely from adult to child, child to adult, as if the channel of communication between these two tribes was untrammelled, unblocked by history, *free*. (p. 319)

Irie's fascination with the Chalfens, however, blinds her to their sanctimonious tendencies, and Joshua's rebellious decision to oppose his father by joining FATE indicates that as a model of cross-generational communication the Chalfens leave much to be desired. The communication between adult and child is just as dictated by history, and no more *"free,"* than in her own family. Marcus's pride in his position as the Chalfen patriarch, though he would certainly not characterize it as such, is not so very different from Archie and Samad's.

The study of generations in *White Teeth* is inseparable from one of gender: Archie and Samad's much younger wives effectively create a generation gap even before the arrival of the children. Alsana's dismissive wit and Clara's more nostalgic love towards their husbands further distances them, isolating Archie and Samad in their world of war anecdotes. Archie and Samad may be patriarchs, but their beliefs are sidelined by their families' vocal interruptions. Alsana's violent and then passive resistance dramatizes the generational and gender conflict of the novel, though Smith's tone directs analysis away from an earnest exploration of the difficulties of familial relationships towards an appreciation of the levity of its thematic treatment.

There are, though, moments of rapprochement. On the bus to the Perret Institute, after Archie's innocent request about why bus tickets contain so much information leads to an almighty family squabble and Irie's outburst, there is such a moment of calm:

"You all right, love?" Archie asked her, after a long period of silence had set in, putting his big pink hand on her knee, dotted with liver-spots like tea-stains. "A lot on your chest, then."

"Fine, Dad. I'm fine."

Archie smiled at her, and tucked a stray hair behind her ear.

"Dad."

"Yes?"

"The thing about the bus tickets."

"Yes?" (p. 516)

As Irie goes on to explain a theory about the bus tickets, and Archie to ponder whether people are less honest than they used to be, father and daughter are brought together in a unit that overcomes gender and generation, even though Archie knows—in his simple way—that he cannot offer Irie the reassurance she seems to be asking for any more than she can explain the London transport system to him. Their momentary union excludes the noise of constant conflict, and while it answers no questions it offers a respite uncommon to their family life, and also to the hectic narrative of White Teeth. As such, contrary to the expectation created by the loquacity of both its cast and its reception, the novel becomes an appeal for calm and the occasional virtues of quietism. This plea is also to be found in the satire on a new Britain in the consumer style questionnaire through which the Perret Institute is envisioned. Rejecting the "renam[ing]" and "rebrand[ing]" of corporate culture, what the immigrant wants is "nothing nothing space please just space nothing please nothing space" (p. 518). The chapter ends with these unpunctuated words, gesturing towards a form of expression beyond fashion, beyond speech.

Chance, Choice, and Fate

White Teeth begins with Archie's attempted suicide. In a typically playful opening paragraph, the narrator details the decision-making process that led Archie to be lying forwards on the steering-wheel, waiting for death to overcome him:

A little green light flashed in his eye, signalling a right turn he had resolved never to make. He was resigned to it. He was prepared for it. He had flipped a coin and stood staunchly by its conclusions. This was a decided-upon suicide. In fact it was a New Year's resolution. (p. 3)

Already, vital elements in Archie's characterization are apparent. The "decided-upon suicide" is in fact a decision taken not by Archie but by the flip of a coin: his decision is to rely on fate. His ironic New Year's resolution indicates Archie's passivity and reliance on chance rather than decision. However, he is not entirely free of agency in his suicide. He is aware that "Cricklewood Broadway would seem a strange choice" of location, but for him "country people should die in the country and city people should die in the city" (p. 3). So he parks his car in a butcher's delivery bay, whose owner will insist that he moves on, and lives:

The thinnest covering of luck was on him like fresh dew. Whilst he slipped in and out of consciousness, the position of the planets, the music of the spheres, the flap of a tiger-moth's diaphanous wings in Central Africa, and a whole bunch of other stuff that Makes Shit Happen had decided it was second-chance time for Archie. Somewhere, somehow, by somebody, it had been decided that he would live. (p. 4)

The combination of luck and his own agency grace Archie with his "second chance," or — given the number of miraculous escapes that Archie makes in the course of the novel — grace him with one of a series of second chances.

The language of chance, choice, and fate is scattered through *White Teeth*, providing both character motivation and thematic debate. When Magid enters O'Connell's after his return from Bangladesh, he asks the assembled company whether he should meet with Millat. Archie, ever non-committal, will not venture an answer despite Samad's frustrated request to him to "'Make a decision, Archibald. For once in your pathetic little life, make a decision'" (p. 457). So he makes his decision the way he habitually does, by flipping a coin. The coin, though, arcs through the air into the slot of the pinball machine, setting off its mechanism, leading Archie not to answer Magid's question, but to ask "'What are the chances of that, eh?'" (p. 457).

The chances are, as the next paragraph suggests, slim. However, the exact verbal repetition of the coin's arc re-enacts the trajectory of an earlier flipped coin, though one that is described later in the novel. In World War II, the Russian soldiers lose Perret to Samad at poker. Samad wants to kill him, both as an "'atonement'" for the fact that they have not killed any of the enemy, and to prevent his eugenics project. Samad declares they are at "'a moral crossroads'" for, if Archie is a character reliant on chance, Samad is beset by choice (p. 118). Samad decides that it will be Archie that will kill Perret, and sends him into the night to commit the deed. Archie, once more confronted with choice, decides to flip the coin whose trajectory foreshadows the one that falls into the pinball machine. This time, though, the consequence of the coin falling behind Archie is that as he turns to pick it up (it is tails: he will not kill the Doctor) Perret grabs the gun Archie has put on the ground, shoots him in the thigh, and disappears into the night. When he reappears as Marcus's aging mentor at the end of the novel, Archie once more receives a bullet in the thigh intended for Perret, though this time it is from Millat's gun.

Patterns of verbal and narrative repetition festoon *White Teeth*, though their purpose is more than merely decorative. Archie's sequence of miraculous escapes is an intrinsic part of his characterization, and include the failed suicide, the moment in the hurricane when he goes to look something up in the dictionary only seconds before a tree crashes into "an absence that was Archie-shaped" (p. 226), and in the war, on his return from a reconnaissance mission and drinking session to the nearby village to find the tank ambushed. Samad shares Archie's luck on this last venture, leaving his more habitual motivation of moral quandary for Archie's second-chance system. Repetition and chance also stud the lives of the separated twins, and in a passage where the narrator draws attention to the similarities in their lives, coincidence develops as a narrative mode.

Further references to chance, choice, and fate are woven through *White Teeth*. O'Connell's is not just a site of refuge from family life, a curious model of multiculturalism and a place where history is debated, but also a gambling den, where Archie and Samad meet to play poker. The Jehovah's Witnesses await their meeting with destiny at the End of the World. Irie struggles to evade the predestination of the past, though both she and Millat are described as being pre-programmed by genetics and family history: Millat's is "an imperative secreted in the genes and the cold steel [of a gun] in his inside pocket [. . .] the answer to a claim made on him long ago. He's a Pandy deep down. And there's mutiny in his blood." Such predestination — "the four-letter F-word. Fate" — also takes on a televisual aspect, "an unstoppable narrative, written, produced and directed by somebody else." Nonetheless, Millat discovers that predestination isn't such an obvious path, as he "sees the great difference between TV and life," and the moral "[c]onsequences" of his acts (pp. 525, 6).

Marcus Chalfen's experiments with FutureMouse, which Magid explains to his brother "'as correcting the Creator's mistakes'" (p. 464), introduces the science of genetics and its role in altering biological futures to the narrative. The name of Joshua's animal rights group is a heavy hint of the themes played out in the novel. The heated and very contemporary debate about genetics and its capacity to change "nature" then parallels the experiment that Samad makes with nature and nurture by sending one of his twins away. The reversal of Samad's expectations indicates to him the futility of attempting to play god, just as the mouse's anthropomorphized escape "through the hands of those who wished to pin it down" questions humanity's ability to control the future (p. 542).

Style

NARRATIVE AND THE NARRATOR

The complex nature of *White Teeth* is dependent not only upon its multicultural and multivocal cast, but also on its multiple time frames and mixture of linear and non-linear narration. This is demonstrated from the opening, which begins with a very specific account of where and when the action is taking place and moves on to an explanation of Archie's decision and his escape from death. The narrative explains the main motivation of the suicide, his re-cuperation of various items from his wife's family (including the Hoover, the tube of which he will use — has already used, in this reversal of chronology — in his suicide attempt) and the instant at which the decision is made to commit suicide by the already men-tioned tossing of a coin. Yet the introduction of Samad and O'Connell's into the plot stays his decision for a while, before the moment arrives when "the pain reached such a piercing level" that he finds himself back in the car as it fills with gas (p. 13). At this point, he undergoes (in a wink to cinematic cliché) the "obligatory flashback of his life to date" (p. 13), which the narrator expands upon, filling in details of his job and personality, his track-cycling glory and including the text of Horst Ibelgaufts' letters. Thus the narrative interweaves moments from past and present, combines dialogue and narrative commentary, and inserts extra-textual mate-rial such as the letters. The description of what is happening, or what has happened, is revised by the narrative transitions, for exam-ple, the finality of "Quietly he detached the Hoover tube, put it in the suitcase, and left the house for the last time" is tempered by the next sentence, "But dying's no easy trick" (p. 11). *White Teeth* is, essentially, a novel based on revision, on the "second chance." It begins with a suicide whose victim is still alive eighteen years later.

Although stretches of *White Teeth* are told according to linear chronology, just as often the narrative goes into reverse, or jumbles the sequence: reversing, restarting, restating, revising. The structure of the novel, as indicated on the contents page, mimics the way-wardness of the narrative. The part titles — "Archie 1974, 1945," "Samad 1984, 1857," "Irie 1990, 1907" and "Magid, Millat and Marcus 1992, 1999" — demonstrate this. Although the named char-acter(s) of each part do feature prominently in that part, it is not exclusively the story of their life (as the "1857" of Samad's section suggests), nor is all of their life included in it. Other patternings occur in the chapter titles, including alliteration, the teeth metaphor and the "root canals," and the stylistic repetition of each of the opening chapters ("The Peculiar Second Marriage of [. . .]," "The Temptation of [. . .]," "The Miseducation of [. . .]" and "The Return of [. . .]"). The novel's thematic concern with history and the inescapability of the past is reflected in the novel's structure, a matching of subject to plot.

With such a profusion of time frames operating within the novel, and variable ways in which they are written (dialogue; free indirect discourse; omniscient and intrusive narration), it is pertinent to ask whether Smith manages to retain control over her narrative. Is the saturation of plotting, and the verbosity of the narrative voice, analogous to Smith's own satirical portrait of Brother Ibrāhīm ad-Din Shukrallah, KEVIN's founder, a man with a "habit of using three words where one would do" (p. 467)? James Wood, in the most thorough critical response to the novel thus far, claimed in *The New Republic* that *White Teeth* suffers from an "excess of storytelling" that privileges plot over characterization. Certainly, the desire for comprehensivity enacted in the narrative leads the plot through not just the back histories of major characters, but also to more anecdotal depictions, such as Brother Ibrāhīm's. The garrulous narrative voice occasionally gives the impression of not knowing when, or how, to stop.

The dénouement is a prime example of the problems of the novel's form. After spanning the twentieth century, after introducing and following the lives of several characters, after declaring its interest in immigrancy, multiculturalism, history, science, and destiny, some attempt at conclusion must be made. The mode that Smith decides upon is that of the grand finale: all the characters, and themes, gathered together in one place, at one time. The rationale for such a gathering is the exposition of Marcus's FutureMouse.

This is a scene of revelation and reconciliation that finds literary precedent in the comedies of Shakespeare, yet whether Smith succeeds in her provision of such an ending is questionable. The final quarter of the novel (the "Magid, Millat and Marcus 1992, 1999" part) could indeed be characterized as a struggle for an ending. The introduction of Marcus's science into the plot, although thematically linked, becomes an overworked (and, in media terms, overexposed) metaphor as well as a facile way of gathering the characters. As the Chaltens are a family already suffering from comic stereotyping, to use them as means of ending the novel further privileges plot over characterization. The novel then risks its carefully built up balance between empathy and commentary, elevating comedy at the expense of complexity. The novel's coda, in which it moves beyond the comic finale to a conditional consideration of 1999, indicates the narrator's own preoccupation that the finale is an inappropriate ending, and will only lead to *"endgames"* rather than the more proper understanding of "the end [a]s simply the beginning of an even longer story" (pp. 540–1). This preoccupation reflects a frustration with fiction's attempts to shape real life, to turn such events as the "independence of India or Jamaica [. . .] the signing of peace treaties or the docking of passenger boats" (all very tellingly events that signal the move from colonial to postcolonial periods) into neat endings (p. 540). The ending of the novel may not be perfect, but this is inherent in the nature of fiction:

But surely to tell these tall tales and others like them would be to speed the myth, the wicked lie, that the past is always tense and the future, perfect. And as Archie knows, it's not like that. It's never been like that. (p. 541)

Resisting the ending thus goes hand in hand with providing the ending, and is part of the novel's thematics. Yet turning the difficulty of creating an ending into a gesture of metanarrativity does not put the novel's negotiation between character and plot beyond reproach.

The failures of this negotiation become most apparent in the character of Clara. She is first thought of by Samad as a hypothetical second bride for Archie, the younger woman who will be to him as Alsana is to Samad. Her first actual appearance is under the guise of an "accident" (p. 23), as she walks into Archie's life at the party, "in slow motion, surrounded by afterglow and fuzzy lighting" (p. 24). The depiction of Clara is one explicitly made with reference to "movies and the like," and the stereotypical entrance of a beautiful female into the plot is satirized as Archie's addled middle-aged perception (p. 24). Yet Clara rarely escapes from others' perceptions in the novel. Her character is very much an adjunct: as wife and mother to Archie and Irie; as the foil to Alsana's scabrous wit. Clara's quieter attempts at diplomacy typically go unheard by the characters and unexplored by the narrator. She has her teeth knocked out in another accident, thus subjecting her jaw to the novel's scheme of metaphors. Neena, Alsana's lesbian "Niece-of-Shame" (p. 63), introduces Clara to "a secret [feminist] lending library" (p. 78), but the fruits of this labor are so underdeveloped that, apart from brief references to evening classes, it comes as a surprise that Clara is able to offer a room for Magid and Millat to meet in her "present seat of learning, a red-brick university, South-West by the Thames" (p. 458). Clara's education is mentioned in passing, its purpose merely to provide a space for other characters' concerns to be played out. It is ironic that Smith, as a young female writer, makes a brief nod to feminism and then leaves Clara without a voice. While this could be seen as typical of the novel's rejection of politically correct representations (Samad's tribulations with his faith being another), it is not sufficiently explored for it to be anything other than a throwaway piece of characterization, an example of the subjugation of character to plot. Moreover, there is not much sense of Clara's interior life built into the narrative, and when insights are offered, they are not entirely convincing. Clara marries Archie, the narrator informs the reader, as a result of her loss of faith, and her wish for a "saviour" (p. 45) in the form of a man:

Perhaps it is not so inexplicable, then, that when Clara Bowden met Archie Jones at the bottom of some stairs the next morning she saw more in him than simply a rather short, rather chubby middle-aged white man in a badly tailored suit. Clara saw Archie through the grey-green eyes of loss; her world had just disappeared, the faith she lived by had receded like a low tide, and Archie, quite by accident, had become the bloke in the joke: the last man on earth. (p. 45)

It is indeed a "Peculiar [. . .] Marriage," as the chapter heading emphasizes in a manoeuvre that, by foregrounding the unbelievability of the act, attempts to stave off criticism of it. Yet the problem is not just the disparity between Clara and Archie—the physical difference that the registrar notes at their wedding—nor the context that is given for Clara's decision, but the manner of its description. Clara's loss of faith, and consequent acceptance of Archie, fails to convince both because of the lack of interiorization of her character, and also because of the comic representation of the Jehovah's Witnesses. Their faith—Clara's faith, until she loses it—is a comic opportunity. Her loss of faith does not work as a convincing motivation because of its representational mode, and the limited space it occupies in the narrative—unlike that granted to Samad's struggles. The "believability" of Clara's motivation hinges, then, on the impact of comic representation. Whether the characters are locked into stereotypes, and the extent to which their actions are reliant on the demands of the plot, is regulated by the novel's genre definition.

The position of the narrator is also instrumental in the negotiation between plot and character. The narrator takes up a variety of positions in the course of the novel, sometimes switching mode within the course of a scene. The first visit to the Chalfen family, and the comments on immigrancy that the narrator makes in response to Joyce's remark about "'strangers,'" is one instance of the switch in narrative position. It moves from a blend of dialogue and omniscient narration to a more explicitly didactic commentary. After Marcus says he has "'to play a bit of piano'" with one of his younger sons, for example, Irie tries to imagine Samad or Archie playing Scott Joplin or helping with biology homework (p. 326). These images, though, are replaced by a figuring of her thoughts that is more metaphorical, more of a narrative imposition than a direct transcription of her interiority: "So there existed fathers who dealt in the present, who didn't drag ancient history around like a chain and ball. So there were men who were not neck-high and sinking in the quagmire of the past." (p. 326). These concerns are recognizably Irie's, and so the narrative shift is not immediately apparent. However, the images of "chain and ball" (the normal inversion of "ball and chain" itself a clue to the narrator's intervention) and "quagmire" are more writerly than a product of Irie's imagination. The change in register is palpable, and heralds the direct intrusion of narrative commentary which follows shortly afterwards. The narrator even addresses the reader through the use of the pronouns "you" and "we," claiming first that "It is only this late in the day, and possibly only in Willesden, that you can find best friends Sita and Sharon [. . .]" (p. 327), and "despite all the mixing up, despite the fact that we have finally slipped into each other's lives [. . .]" (p. 327). The appeal to the reader through direct address and inclusive pronouns marks the most intrusive level of the narrative voice. The narrator self-consciously steps into the action, comments upon it, and draws in the reader. The effect of the changing position of the narrator is to create a fluctuating tone, particularly in the creation of character: sometimes an empathetic interiorization, sometimes a comic exteriorization, and sometimes a contextualising voice of authority.

VOICE

In the midst of "Samad 1984, 1857," the narrative pauses to consider the effects of Samad's decision to separate his twin sons. Magid has broken his nose in a freak accident, a vase dislodged by a cyclone falling on him from a shelf in a mosque (the narrator steps in and intrusively asks the reader to "keep one eye on that vase, please" [p. 213]). The Iqbals then receive a letter and photo from Magid and, as a result of his father's miscomprehension of "the language of the Willesden streets," Millat laughs so hard that he falls and breaks *his* nose on a sink (p. 216). This double nose-breaking, so the twins once more look identical, leads the narrator to a reflection on the separate but connected development of the twins. The elements of coincidence in the twins' lives are explored by the narrator, in a voice that both informs and teases the reader, extending authority, interrogating authority, and hence foregrounding the narrative's fictionality:

And Alsana only knew the incidentals: similar illnesses, simultaneous accidents, pets dying continents apart. She did not know that while Magid watched the 1985 cyclone shake things from high places, Millat was pushing his luck along the towering wall of the cemetery in Fortune Green; [. . .] Ah, but you are not convinced by coincidence? You want fact fact fact? You want brushes with the Big Man with the black hood and scythe? OK: on the 28th April, 1989, a tornado whisked the Chittagong kitchen up into the sky, taking everything with it except Magid, left miraculously curled up in a ball on the floor. Now, segue to Millat, five thousand miles away, lowering himself down upon legendary sixth-former Natalia Cavendish (whose body is keeping a dark secret from her); the condoms are unopened in a box in his back pocket; but somehow he will not catch it; even though he is moving rhythmically now, up and in, deeper and sideways, dancing with death. (p. 220)

Omniscience is signaled both by the authority with which Magid and Millat's joint destinies are brought together, an omniscience that goes beyond Alsana's knowledge, and, even more emphatically, beyond Natalia Cavendish's, a character who never reappears in the novel but whose future is mapped out by this briefest of narrative asides. Built into this omniscience, though, is an assumption of the reader's position, as the narrator seems to provide a response to an off-page expression of disbelief. The assumption of the reader's disbelief, however, foregrounds the fictionality of the work, making a challenge to the actual reader not to identify with the "you" of the implied reader, but rather to develop a discerning stance towards the narrative voice's coercion of character.

The narrative garrulity of *White Teeth* intensifies its coercive force. Irie, considering Joshua's transition from Chalfen to animal rights activist, is described as:

[not] surprised by Joshua's metamorphosis. Four months in the life of a seventeen-year-old is the stuff of swings and roundabouts; Stones fans into Beatles fans, Tories into Liberal Democrats and back again, vinyl junkies to CD freaks. Never again in your life do you possess the capacity for such total personality overhaul. (p. 404)

This passage, like the earlier section when she encounters the Chalfens, starts with Irie's thoughts, but then is taken up in a narrative riff of analogy and metaphor, and concludes with a sentence that sounds most unlike the product of Irie's mind. A more extreme example of narrative digression is the introduction of the story of the "Queen of Thailand" into the plot, in order to illustrate impact of tradition (p. 193). The story has no purpose other than that of analogy, and contributes more to a superfluity of image than a real understanding of Samad's motivation. Such passages, although diverting and indicative of the engaging narrative largesse, endanger its sense of purpose. When Smith provides the narrator with a string of synonyms for "immigrants ('fugees, émigrés, travellers)," she falls prey to her own satire on the very next page, Brother Ibrāhīm's thesaurus tendency to "'elucidate, explain and *expound* . . .'" when just one of the verbs would do (p. 467).

Tautology, and the garrulous narrator, are symptoms of Smith's inexperience as a writer. As Smith herself has stated, the novel could perhaps have merited from more incisive editing at points such as these. Nonetheless, they are also symptoms of the depth and range of her reference, of a writer brimming with ideas but not always with an adequate control over them. To mitigate further, the garrulous narrator is a fictional trope appearing in works ranging from Laurence Sterne's *Tristram Shandy* to Rushdie's *Midnight's Children*. It shifts the novel from realism into other genres, heralds its fictionality, and also, in its more accomplished examples—among which *White Teeth* can be counted—impresses and delights with its inventive energies. Yet it is also, inherently, a risky strategy: the author may intentionally satirize the narrator, but may wound him or herself in the process. In *White Teeth*, the plea for "a bit of silence, a bit of *shush*" (p. 4) is arguably the most heartfelt of the novel, but it battles against the insistent chatter of the narrative.

The voicing of different characters and their ethnic groups is one of the most apparent features of *White Teeth*. From Archie's bumbling homilies to the "appalling pronunciation" of the customers Samad takes orders from in the restaurant (p. 55), from Alsana's wacky images to the hybrid street slang of the "*Raggastani*," and from Irie's rising, soap-opera influenced, Antipodean intonation (p. 377) to her accusation that Millat's Caribbean-toned speech is "'not your voice. You sound ridiculous!'" (p. 239) Smith displays a finely-tuned ear for linguistic inflections and their sociocultural nuances. *White Teeth* is thus turned into an aural experience, whose comedy is better transmitted by the voice than the page. Ventriloquism is a central comic effect, although the play of textuality—the very Shandean diagrams, equations, and charts that litter the novel—also emphasizes the importance of the written page in the construction of its humor.

Verbal and narrative patterns of repetition occur throughout *White Teeth*. The impact of this is on both the novel's themes and its characterization. The narrator, for example, considers Archie's post-suicide "second chance":

a new Archie is about to emerge. We have caught him on the hop. For he is in a past-tense, future-perfect kind of mood. He is in a *maybe this, maybe that* kind of mood. (p. 18)

Early on in the novel, two of the recurring phrases ("past-tense, future-perfect," "*maybe this, maybe that*") of the novel are used. The latter, as Alsana's key phrase of passive resistance, is a particularly interesting transposition, as it implies a linguistic texture to the novel that permeates the consciousness of various characters as well as the narrator, slipping between individuals to create an organic identity underpinning them all. This linguistic transposition has a dual effect. First, it locks characters in, subsuming them to the greater narrative drive. This is an imprisonment of sorts, another example of the subjugation of character to plot. However, it also lends a coherency to the novel, a way of uniting the disparate characters and stories of the plot in an alternative to the grand finale. From the very beginning, in other words, the characters and their stories are linked through the textual strategies of the novel, rather than relying on the more torturous plot development of FutureMouse. These strategies are linked to the themes of coincidence and chance, and the embrace they extend to the reader is that of genre definition.

GENRE

The passage describing Magid and Millat's intertwined destinies includes a moment when Magid is in a Bangladeshi cyclone, while Millat teeters on top of a London wall. It is these coincidences that set the narrative teetering between genre definitions. Elements of the fantastic combine with recognizable locations; and real historical events are woven into the kaleidoscopic patterns of linguistic and plot repetition. The novel's historiographical concerns point towards a definition of *White Teeth* as a metanarrative. Its commentary upon its own narrative method asserts this, and its structure of teeth metaphors substantiates it. Yet the self-reflexivity, although sometimes too digressional, is rarely narcissistic in *White Teeth*, indeed its negotiation between the modes of realism and magic realism lends the narrative its generous, inclusive tone. The coincidences in the twins' lives, and the linguistic and plot repetitions, are rendered believable within the ambit of the narrative. The real-life "coincidences" frequently reported in the lives of twins also support the believability of Magid and Millat's linked fates, but they are mainly sustained on a textual level. The fantastic elements of the plot often function more convincingly than the supposedly psychological interpretations proffered for choices made by characters.

The crisis in representing character motivation is not one between realism and magic realism, then, which are comfortable companions in the novel. Rather, there is a strain in the comic representations that sometimes relies too heavily on stereotype. The Chalfens are the obvious victims, while the humor at the expense of the Jehovah's Witnesses belittles the development of Clara's motivations. This is not to suggest that *White Teeth* is a failure as a comic novel, but that it has serious flaws, not the least of which is the surrender of characterization to stereotype and the cheap one-liner. Humorous elements such as the slapstick domestic violence between Samad and Alsana and the depiction of racism are much more successful manifestations of the comic mode in *White Teeth*, demonstrating a more delicate understanding of the interplay between comedy, reality, and political judgement. That Smith can treat her characters with empathy while avoiding the sanctimony of political correctness sees her performing one of the most delicate transactions a novelist can make, and when she succeeds it elevates her novel far above the majority of contemporary fictions. The satirical impact of the novel is thus sharpened, while the value of sheer entertainment is never forgotten.

The broad sweep of the novel, its portrait of the twentieth century from beginning to end, its incorporation of actual events into fictional narrative, and its engagement with the urgent postcolonial themes of immigrancy and multiculturalism, suggest another definition for *White Teeth*: that of the historical novel. Yet if the novel continues to be read in years to come, it will not be for its portrayal of World War II and Jamaica at the turn of the century, but for its representation of the London of the 1970s, 1980s and 1990s. Its treatment of this period and place has, since its publication, made it a fashionable book, reflective of the zeitgeist and articulate about the emergent state of the contemporary nation. If, in the future, however, *White Teeth* is still considered an important novel to read, it will inevitably be at the loss of its modish trappings but in favor of qualities that have more longevity: the accomplishment of its artistic endeavor; its bravura capacity to entertain and provoke; and, not least, its very human concern with how we are to understand our past, live in our present and create our futures.

3

The Novel's Reception

White Teeth's publication in the U.K. was heralded by a high level of pre-publication publicity, including mentions of the advance deal, profiles of the author, and an extract in *Granta*. Salman Rushdie made one of the earliest critical commentaries on the novel, which was included in the jacket copy and thus incorporated into the marketing of the book. His very positive statement set the agenda for the book's reception. U.S. publication, though not so heavily foreshadowed, did follow Smith's appearance in the *New Yorker*'s Millennial Fiction issue.

Initial reviews of *White Teeth* inevitably demonstrated an awareness of the hype that attended the novel's publication. As well as reviews, interviews with the author formed a substantial part of the coverage received by *White Teeth*. The effect this would have on the reception of *White Teeth* would be to foreground autobiographical issues in relation to the novel, despite the assertion of many reviewers that it lacked the self-regarding turn of many first-time novelists. Smith's relative youth, her mixed-race background and her connection to the locales of *White Teeth* were all put under the microscope. In the book's development as one of the first publishing phenomena of the 21st century, such examinations were crucial.

The reviewers had to negotiate their way past the excitement generated by such contextual readings in order to arrive at more considered opinions of the text itself. Anne Chisholm in the *Sunday Telegraph*, Hugo Barnacle in the *Sunday Times* and Ali Smith in the *Scotsman* all prefaced their reviews with reference to the publicity surrounding the book, Chisholm actually quoting from the publishers' press release. The assertions that these reviewers made were based on a measurement of the novel's achievements against the claims made for it by the publishers and the amount of pre-publication coverage, Chisholm asserting that "For once, the hype is justified," and Ali Smith claiming that "This is a prodigious novel [. . .] It would have to be [. . .], just to live up to the several years' hype this first novel has already had."

Other critics of *White Teeth* did not frame their analysis so blatantly in the context of the hype, although their awareness of these contexts can be assumed. The prevailing note of the reception of *White Teeth*, though, has been one of exceptional praise. For Caryl Phillips in the *Observer*, *White Teeth* was "restless and wonderfully poised" and "audaciously assured." Melissa Denes in the *Daily Telegraph* thought it "bounding, vibrant, richly imagined and thoroughly engaging." Lisa Allardice in the London *Evening Standard* termed it "an ambitious first novel, [. . .] she pulls [. . .] off magnificently." For Maya Jaggi in the *Guardian* it was "a serio-comic novel of great verve and distinction." Anne Chisholm went on in her review to call it "a strikingly clever and funny book with a passion for ideas, for language and for the rich tragi-comedy of life [. . .] outstanding." Hugo Barnacle viewed it as a "fluent, observant, deeply amiable novel." Ali Smith's paean saw it as "a book so readable and good-hearted [with] a vision [. . .] so clever and encompassing [. . .] a book full of admirable energy and salvaged joie de vivre, a truly epic, shining piece of life."

The U.S. reviews continued the cavalcade of praise for *White Teeth*. The *New York Times*'s reviewer, Michiko Kakutani, described it as "a novel that announces the debut of a preternaturally gifted new writer—a writer who at the age of 24 demonstrates both an instinctive storytelling talent and a fully fashioned voice that's street-smart and learned, sassy and philosophical all at the same time [. . .] Smith announces herself as a writer of remarkable powers, a writer whose talents prove commensurate with her ambitions." Jane Vandenburgh of the *Boston Globe* categorized the book as "a masterpiece." Mark Rozzo in the *Los Angeles Times* termed it a "dazzling intergenerational first novel," claiming that "Smith is already a wonderfully inventive synthesizer of ideas and a master of style whose prose is playful yet unaffected, mongrel yet cohesive, profound yet funny, vernacular yet lyrical." Dan Cryer in *Newsday* thought it "an extraordinary book by an extraordinary talent [. . .] enchantment conveyed on a large canvas by a gifted storyteller." Greg Tate in the *Village Voice* alluded to the author of *Gravity's Rainbow* (1973) and *V* (1963) in seeing "*White Teeth* [as] virtuosic and prodigious beyond belief in its command of epic and epoch-raiding Pynchonesque novelistic technique [. . .] a grand and masterful performance." Such enthusiastic commentary inexorably made its way onto the paperback editions of the novel.

Yet despite the overwhelmingly positive critical reception of *White Teeth*, it was not entirely uniform. Among reviewers of the novel, there were voices of dissent, and many of the adjectivally rapturous did also insert words of reserve into their praise. One of the most common complaints stemmed from what has also been seen as one of the virtues of Smith's writing. Although the linguistic play of *White Teeth* was admired, some also thought it occasionally out of control. Ali Smith, for example, wrote that "The writing is all brio, relentlessly witty. Something of this quippy relentlessness makes *White Teeth* a bit of a sprawl, gives it a texture sometimes too fast for itself." Lisa Allardice stated that "Her rather volcanic style, while overflowing with talent, might have benefited from more ruthless editing." Allardice, writing in *The Times* on the paperback publication of the book, extended her critique, saying that, "There are flaws. The book is too long and untamed. It works better as a novel of ideas and a noisy, colourful celebration of contemporary London than as a conventional narrative. Towards the end it falls away with a clumsy denouement designed to unite all the storylines and themes."

The manner in which the novel ends proved of concern to several reviewers. The finale was thought to be a "contrived, altogether unsatisfying resolution that tries to pick up all the scattered pieces at once" by John Gamino in the *Dallas Morning News*. Although almost universally applauded for creating and maintaining a complex narrative line and multiple character perspectives, the attempt to bring them all together at the end clearly prompted differing reactions. Ali Smith, for example, in contradiction to Gamino and Allardice, thought "Smith pulls it all off with an ending nothing short of glorious."

Characterization also proved to be an aspect of *White Teeth* that divided the critical response, although Smith's ear for the speech patterns of her characters was generally applauded. The debate centered on whether the characters were allowed to escape their representative status to become fully-rounded creations. Michiko Kakutani thought they did, claiming that, "These characters are all players in [...] Smith's riotous multicultural drama, living out their stories on her chessboard of postcolonial dreams and frustrations, and yet at the same time, they've been limned with such energy and bemused affection that they possess the quirks and vulnerabilities of friends and neighbors we've known all our lives." Other critics were less convinced, including Beatrice Colin of Scotland's *Sunday Herald*, who believed Smith's "descriptions of her main protagonists are exceptional, astute and acutely well observed, but that's the problem. They're only descriptions, we never get under their skins and we are only allowed to observe [. . .] Without living, breathing, developing characters, it doesn't take long before Smith has to resort to some convoluted and contrived plotting simply to reach a conclusion." The Chalfen family were a particular source of contention, with several reviewers thinking them drawn too much for comic effect to have an existence beyond stereotype.

Satire was seen as a prevalent mode by some reviewers, with Sukhdev Sandhu in the *Times Literary Supplement* pronouncing the novel's similarity in scope to Jonathan Coe's state-of-the-nation *What a Carve Up!* (1994). U.S. reviewers, including Dan Cryer, were keen to define the satire as a particularly British mode, in the manner of Charles Dickens and William Thackeray: "her ebullient humor, compassion for her characters and outrage at social injustice place her squarely in the Dickensian tradition." Yet *White Teeth*'s satire was also seen as turning the characters into caricatures who were overly controlled by their creator. Daniel Soar in the *London Review of Books* was very much of this opinion, and James Wood in *The New Republic* professed a similar reservation.

Wood's article, the most interesting and extended critique of the novel to appear so far, addresses not only *White Teeth* but several recent fictions, including Rushdie's *The Ground Beneath her Feet* (1999), Thomas Pynchon's *Mason & Dixon* (1997), Don DeLillo's *Underworld* (1997), and David Foster Wallace's *Infinite Jest* (1996). These fictions are described as examples of "the big contemporary novel" which takes Dickens as its progenitor and the dynamics of the "perpetual-motion machine" as its model. The operational mode of these fictions is not magic realism but what Wood terms "hysterical realism," in which the novels' characters are trapped in a series of endless parallels and "connectedness." This "excess of storytelling," which *White Teeth* partakes of in Irie Jones's twin impregnation, for example, and the "clashing finale" of the closing scene, is essentially a result of "the crisis of character" that Wood perceives since Modernism. Although Smith is not the most guilty of the authors Wood examines, he suggests that "her principal characters move in and out of human depth. Sometimes they seem to provoke her sympathy, at other times they are only externally comic." This leads to an over-reliance on plot rather than character-ization, of novels "in the paradoxical position of enforcing connec-tions that are finally conceptual rather than human." Wood's thesis is that these fictions fail to create believable characters and situa-tions, even with the frame of their fictionality. Analyzing Smith's depiction of the founder of KEVIN, Woods argues of *White Teeth* that "as realism, it is incredible; as satire, it is cartoonish; as cartoon, it is too realistic [. . .] It is all shiny externality, all caricature." The legacy of Dickens is thus "that a large part of characterization *is* merely the management of caricature." Wood's impressed yet criti-cal reading of Smith's characterization notes how it veers from internal to external representation, "a curious shuffle of sympathy and distance, affiliation and divorce, brilliance and cartoonishness, astonishing maturity and ordinary puerility." The unevenness of her portrayal is, Wood hopes, a sign of Smith's youth, and it is in her future work that "glamorous congestion" should be rejected for the more gentle lessons that Dickens can instill.

The question of influence and allegiance preoccupied many of *White Teeth*'s reviewers. Dickens was named by many, though more as a comparison for Smith's portrayal of London than as a sustained argument about her characterization. Martin Amis's metropolitan depictions in novels such as *London Fields* (1989) were also seen as a precedent. The ghosts of Thackeray and Laurence Sterne were invoked, the former for his satire, the latter for his narrative digressions and typographical experimentation. The Rushdie and Kureishi connection was widely mentioned. Sukhdev Sandhu, for example, thought that "A belief in contingency, the tricksy messiness of our lives, aligns *White Teeth* with a novel such as *The Satanic Verses*. And in her fascination with the unholy metropolis, the trans-histories and cross-continentalizing of its inhabitants, as well as her alertness to the uses and creative abuses of the past, Smith's writing has a good deal in common with Rushdie's." Maya Jaggi extended the frame of reference to include cultural commentators as well as postcolonial novelists. Smith, she declared, "is steeped in her fore-runners. She has imbibed Edward Said [. . .], while Salman Rush-die's influence pervades the chattily intrusive narrative voice. And whether pilfering or in playful homage, the novel carries echoes from the migrant, or 'post-immigrant', literatures of such as Sam Selvon, Caryl Phillips, Michael Ondaatje, and Hanif Kureishi."

Without exception, every critic of *White Teeth* has referred to the novel's treatment of multiculturalism. For many, it is this that lends the novel its energy. Allardice's *Evening Standard* review, for example, commented that *White Teeth* is "[t]eeming with characters, their tangled histories and conflicting beliefs, [it] captures the colourful multicultural landscape of London." Christopher Mat-thew and Hephzibah Anderson in the *Daily Mail* praised it as "a playful, refreshingly upbeat portrait of multicultural Britain." Sarah Sands in the *Daily Telegraph*, with an ear well-attuned to the sound-bite, termed Smith "a George Eliot of multi-culturalism." More open to debate, though, was the question of whether Smith was portraying an actual or an ideal situation. John Lanchester in *The New York Review of Books*, for example, commented that "The version of race relations it describes is utopian, a vision of how things might be rather than how they are." To Lanchester's mind, the London of *White Teeth* was "optimistically reimagined". The novel's appeal was analyzed as at least partly a result of its optimistic spirit. Some, though, questioned both the actuality and viability of the novel's utopian vision. Wood worried that the multiculturalism of *White Teeth* was not so much a political statement, or an actual depiction of immigrant communities, but an artificial way of connecting plot and character, "a formal lesson rather [than] an actual enactment." Greg Tate wrote that *White Teeth* "seems, for all its heft and multiple cultural perspectives, remarkably slight, if not evasive, on the matter of how people of African and Afro-Caribbean descent interact with one another on British soil." The accusation of "slightness" merits further consideration: numerous critics noted the weighty subject matter of the novel but expressed their concern that Smith's discussion of it could sometimes verge on the glib. Several critics interrogated the closing words of the novel. While Smith denies a rose-tinted vision of multiculturalism, Melissa Denes thought "there is something too pat (and too punning) in the conclusion that we should not perpetuate 'the myth, the wicked lie, that the past is always tense and the future, perfect'."

Esther Iverem in the *Washington Post* questioned Smith's authorial stance, seeing her as "both resident and voyeur" of "the multicultural universe." This dual positioning is analogous to the "curious shuffle" that James Wood perceived Smith to be performing. Others, however, have been more complimentary about Smith's comprehension of the complexities of multiculturalism. Caryl Phillips was glowing in his approbation for this aspect of *White Teeth*. Although unconvinced by the caricature of the Chalfens, he stated that "There is nothing farcical about the pain of wanting to belong. In this respect, *White Teeth* is full of false smiles and contrived faces, masks that are repeatedly donned in order to better hide the pain. The 'mongrel' nation that is Britain is still struggling to find a way to stare into the mirror and accept the ebb and flow of history that has produced this fortuitously diverse condition and its concomitant pain [. . .] *White Teeth* squares up to the two questions which gnaw at the very roots of our modern condition: Who are we? Why are we here?" Lynell George in the *Los Angeles Times* believed Smith to be a shrewd analyst of multi-ethnicity: "Those cultural collisions [on the streets of North London] point up an issue often sidestepped — that the melting pot has long been an imperfect metaphor, and that constructing identity is less about [. . .] melting down [. . .] than it is about understanding how to 'add on' and the complications implicit in that task."

Smith's novel came to be seen as having a representative force beyond the limits of its own fictional frame: as having something to say about the condition of modern British society. This aspect of the novel was noted both in the U.K. and the U.S. However, there was some disparity between the reception of *White Teeth* on either side of the Atlantic. Greg Tate's remark about Smith's evasiveness on the issue of African and Afro-Caribbean experience in London is indicative of a greater level of interest in the U.S. in Smith as a black author describing black experience, rather than as a mixed-race writer depicting a multicultural environment. U.K. reviews concentrated more on the Iqbals — and the aspects of faith and fundamentalism that the Muslim family illustrate — than on Clara's Jamaican family. Esther Iverem went so far as to say that she felt the blacks in *White Teeth* were made to "serve as a convenient sideshow". More favorable mentions of Smith as a black writer appeared, for example in Miles Marshall Lewis's article "The Black Book" in the *Village Voice*, but what is perhaps most striking is the conscription (or rejection) of Smith to the cause of black writing. It is a cause Smith has rejected herself, but also one about which the question of autobiographical interpretation should be demanded. In an interview in *Time*, Nadya Labi suggested that Smith attempted to write a novel that "transcends her personal demographics". Smith is quoted in Labi's article as saying, "'A lot of black writing is this love-in, and I definitely don't write love-ins [. . .] What did people think I was going to write? Some kind of searing slave drama or single-girl-in-London tale?'"

Smith's question, and the criticism it makes of autobiographical interpretations and expectations of writers, is wholly pertinent to the reception of her novel. While reviewers did not always fall into the trap of defining her work through her ethnicity, the profile writers were certainly fascinated by it, and as such increased the media attention paid to the novel. Moreover, even the most circumspect of reviews had a sense of Smith's youth. Melissa Denes was perhaps disingenuous when she wrote that "it would not matter if she were a he, white and the wrong side of 40: Smith can write." Much of the reception of *White Teeth* was quite properly aware that it was a novel written by an author at the beginning of her career and so, as well as commenting upon the novel itself, the critics excused or compensated for the errors of youth, and lauded the capacities for development. In the final analysis, it is this that explains the excitement of the reception to *White Teeth*: that it is a novel that holds out great promise for the future of its author and her readers.

4

The Novel's Performance

In the months following its publication, *White Teeth* became a big commercial as well as critical success. In its U.K. and U.S. hardback and paperback editions it has sold over a million copies, and the novel has dominated the bestseller lists on both sides of the Atlantic. To give an indication of the novel's sales tenacity, in the week of the U.K. paperback publication in January 2001, the hardback edition was still figuring in the hardback top 10. Foreign rights in the novel have been sold in numerous territories around the world, with France, Germany, Italy, Japan, Sweden, Turkey, and Brazil representing only a proportion of the countries in which the novel would appear.

Television rights for *White Teeth* were won by Company Pictures shortly after publication of the book. A four-part series of one-hour episodes is planned, splitting the novel into the chronological stretches of the 1970s, the 1980s, and then the final two programs on the 1990s. Britain's Channel Four will screen the dramatization in Autumn 2002. It will be directed by Julian Jarrold and will star Om Puri as Samad and Phil Davis as Archie.

White Teeth has also been honored with a substantial number of prizes and awards. In April 2000, it was shortlisted for the women-only Orange Prize, but lost out to Linda Grant's *When I Lived in Modern Times* (2000). Despite being strongly tipped to win the Booker Prize, though, *White Teeth* was not even shortlisted, causing consternation amongst some of the many advocates of the novel. David Robson, commenting in the *Sunday Telegraph* upon the novel's omission, expressed his discontent at the judges' shortlist, concerned that if the "best six British novels in the year of the Millennium are looking back rather than forward, it augurs ill for the future." Smith's novel came to represent the future of the British novel, and its exclusion from Britain's highest-profile prize was indicative, to some commentators, of the backwards-looking nature of the literary establishment. However, *White Teeth* was shortlisted — and won — other prizes, including the Whitbread First Novel Award. The Whitbread judging panel called it "A landmark novel for multicultural Britain, as well as a superb portrait of contemporary London [. . .] Not only the best first novel we've read in ages, but one of the best novels we've ever read, and perhaps the best about contemporary London."

White Teeth went on to become the overall winner of several awards, including the *Guardian* First Book Prize. The judges who awarded Smith the Commonwealth Writers Best First Book Prize repeated many of the journalists' accolades in their statement that "*White Teeth* is an astonishingly attractive debut novel — a most fetching examination of the interlocking lives of immigrant families [. . .] the novel is a wonderfully expansive, inventive, exuberant, comic celebration of multicultural life, growing up, survival, in what it calls the 'mad city' of the English capital." Their enthusiasm was shared by other judges, as it also won the James Tait Black Memorial Prize for Fiction, the WHSmith Book Award for New Talent (voted for by the public from a suggested shortlist), a Betty

Trask Award (for first novels of "a romantic or traditional nature"), and the inaugural fiction prize of the International Ebook awards, for works converted from print into electronic form. The annual publishing industry awards ceremony, the British Book Awards, feted Smith with the title Best Newcomer. She also gained two EMMAs (Ethnic and Multicultural Media Awards), for Best Book and again for Best Newcomer. *White Teeth* has also been shortlisted for the Authors' Club First Novel Award, the South Bank Show Award for Literature and the Mail on Sunday/John Llewellyn Rhys Prize. In the U.S., the novel was shortlisted for the National Book Critics Circle Awards and the *Los Angeles Times* Book Awards. *White Teeth*, then, is a novel that has been garlanded with prizes, increasing both its profile and its literary reputation. It was also granted an auxiliary prize, in the award by the Publishers' Publicity Circle to Hamish Hamilton's publicist. The award was very apposite, for the novel's publicity campaign was crucial in turning it from a success into a phenomenon.

Since its publication, *White Teeth* and its author have come to be seen as representative, illustrating themes and concerns of contemporary British society and also exemplifying aspects of the publishing industry. In an article by Fiachra Gibbons in the *Guardian* entitled "The route to literary success: be young, gifted and very good looking," for example, Smith is touted, along with high-flying peers, as "cool and fashionable—the most marketable." In equal measure, such reports revel in these young literary celebrities and express anxiety for an industry that seems to emphasize qualities which are not purely literary.

For Smith, though, such journalistic attention is a complement to the critical acclaim she has received, and also to her work being seen as an example of the zeitgeist, a new, multicultural, multicolored Britain. This is the Zadie Smith with "demographics at her fingertips," as Sarah Sands put it in the *Daily Telegraph*, and the vision of optimistic social mixing that is to be found in the pages of *White Teeth* is taken as a blueprint for a new Britain. Yet *White Teeth* itself is cautious of such easy definitions. In the final scene at the Perret Institute, Smith's satire on the vacuous signifiers of branding stresses the importance of remembering the humanity of individuals, their long histories and how they find and fit into the spaces of the world:

people can finally give the answers required when a space is being designed, or when something is being rebranded, a room/furniture/Britain (that was the brief: a new British room, a space for Britain, Britishness, space of Britain, British industrial space cultural space space); they know what is meant when asked how matt chrome makes them feel; and they know what is meant by national identity? symbols? paintings? maps? music? air-conditioning? smiling black children or smiling Chinese children or [tick the box]? world music? shag or pile? tile or floorboards? plants? running water?

they know what they want, especially those who've lived this century, forced from one space to another like Mr De Winter (né Wojciech), renamed, rebranded, the answer to every questionnaire nothing nothing space please just space nothing please nothing space (pp. 518–9)

In the end, it is perhaps this that makes *White Teeth* a book of great merit and thus worthy of serious consideration: for its awareness of the difficulties of creating a multicultural society in the face of prejudice, bureaucracy and double-speak; and its celebration of the attempts of ordinary people, with extraordinary lives, to do so.

5

Further Reading and Discussion Questions

In this section, you will find a series of questions and discussion topics on *White Teeth*. Some of these relate to points that have been raised in the previous chapters, while others give some ideas for your own exploration. There are also some suggestions for further reading, including other creative works that make interesting comparisons to *White Teeth*, and works of non-fiction that illuminate the novel's contexts. The section ends with a bibliography of Smith's work and selected criticism and interviews.

QUESTIONS AND DISCUSSION TOPICS

The Past

1. *White Teeth* is prefaced by the quotation "What's past is prologue". In what sense does the past influence the present — and the future — in the novel? How are the younger generations in the novel — Irie, Magid, Millat, Josh — affected by the lives of their parents and grandparents? Is it possible to make a break from the past, and start afresh?

2. One of the legacies in the novel is that made by the British Empire. What is its effect on the characters of the novel, and what is its impact upon the London of the 1970s, 1980s and 1990s? Does it make sense to call London a "postcolonial" city, and *White Teeth* a "postcolonial" novel?

3. Some critics of *White Teeth* have suggested that the more impressive sections of the novel are those set nearer to the present day. Do you agree? How convinced are you by Smith's portrayal of earlier periods and her incorporation of them into the plot of the novel? What does "the much neglected, 100-year-old, mildewed yarn" of Mangal Pande make us think about the past, and about Samad?

Teeth

4. Why is the novel called *White Teeth*? Think of the many references to teeth, including Clara's teeth knocked out in a scooter accident, Irie's decision to become a dentist, and Alsana's description of the Chalfens as "'birds with teeth, with sharp little canines — they don't just steal, they rip apart!'" (p. 344). What are the various meanings of teeth in the novel?

5. When Irie, Magid and Millat visit an old age pensioner with Harvest Festival gifts, he tells them about his experiences in the Congo. How does Mr. J. P. Hamilton's story link white teeth to a history of Empire and racist attitudes? What is the effect of his story on the children? When Millat responds by saying that his father was a war hero for the British army, how do the children, and you, react to Mr. J. P. Hamilton telling Millat that "'Fibs will rot your teeth'" (p. 173)?

6. How do teeth and "root canals" function as a way of constructing history in the novel? How effective are Smith's teeth as a

device for constructing the past? Other novelists have created comparable devices and metaphors for the way in which the past is introduced to their books, including Salman Rushdie's idea of "chutnification"—history made like chutney—in *Midnight's Children*. Can you think of other examples? Do these methods make us rethink the way that history is told?

Family Trees, Roots, and Tradition

7. On the wall of Marcus's study hangs the Chalfen family tree, "an elaborate illustrated oak that stretched back into the 1600s and forward into the present day" (p. 337). Looking at the tree, Irie thinks about her own family history, and a comic tree for the Bowdens is inserted on the page, which features illegitimacy, miscegenation and a very vague sense of time (p. 338). What do the family trees of the different families in the novel tell us about them? What is the importance of heredity? The teenage Irie is "unwilling to settle for genetic fate" (p. 266), desperate to change her body shape and rid herself of "that swollen enormity, the Jamaican posterior" (p. 265). How does Smith combine the science of genetics and the weight of family and cultural tradition in *White Teeth*? What is the impact of emigration on this dual inheritance? Why does Irie want to "merge with the Chalfens, to be of one flesh" (p. 342)?

8. How do the London immigrants negotiate their uprooting? How do their journeys affect their culture, religion and traditions? Why might this be seen, as Irie puts it, as a "'huge battle between who they are and who they should be, what they were and what they will be'"? What differences are there between first and second generation immigrants in the novel, and the ways in which they adapt to their environment? Why does

Smith use the politician Norman Tebbit's statement about "the cricket test" as an epigraph to "Samad 1984, 1857"?

Science and Religion

9. In *White Teeth*, Samad is very concerned about the effect that growing up in Britain has on his family and relations: "'People call it assimilation when it is nothing but corruption. Corruption!'" What are the various different religions represented in the novel? In what ways do characters in the novel have their religious beliefs and customs challenged? What do you think of the tone Smith uses to portray the different groups? Some of the portrayals are comic: do you think this is appropriate? Does she poke fun at some groups more than others? (Think about KEVIN, the Jehovah's Witnesses and the creed of "Chalfenism" as well as the more conventional groups.)

10. Millat goes on an outing with friends to Bradford, where they become involved in protests against a book. The book and author are not named, but from the historical context it is clear that this is Salman Rushdie's *The Satanic Verses*. Why has Smith included this incident in her narrative? Fictionalized versions of *The Satanic Verses* affair also occur in Kureishi's *The Black Album* and David Caute's *Fatima's Scarf*. How do these novels compare to *White Teeth*?

11. Samad's concern with the "corruption" of his children leads him to send Magid back to Bangladesh. What are the implications of this action? How does it affect Magid and Millat's approach to religion? Is this what Samad, or the reader of *White Teeth*, expects? How do the lives of the twins develop in parallel, and in what ways do they differ? In what ways is Smith playing with the scientific debate about nature vs. nurture, and in what ways is she drawing on more literary conventions?

12. What is the role of Marcus's FutureMouse in *White Teeth*? How does it fit the themes of multiculturalism and immigrancy? In what ways is Samad's separation of the two genetically-identical twins a similar experiment to those being carried out by Marcus? Is the combination of these themes an artistically satisfying one?

Multiculturalism

13. *White Teeth* has been widely praised for its portrayal of multicultural London. Do you think this praise was deserved? What is distinctive about Smith's representation of multicultural life? Many critics have commented upon the range of characters and voices that Smith takes on in the novel. Are you impressed by Smith's capacity for ventriloquism in *White Teeth*? Are some of the voices more convincing than others?

14. Do you think Smith is portraying an actual or ideal version of multicultural society? How does the Britain she writes about fit with your experience and knowledge? Racism makes only occasional appearances in the novel, and is often comic in form or deflated in its impact, for example, in Archie's boss asking him not to come with Clara to the works dinner rather than sacking him. What other examples are there of racism or racist attitudes in *White Teeth*? What is the impact of racism on the characters? Is there any connection between racism and the patronising views that Joyce has towards Millat and Irie's families?

15. How do other writers' representations of multicultural Britain compare with Smith's? Some examples you could look at include Salman Rushdie's *The Satanic Verses*, Hanif Kureishi's *The Buddha of Suburbia* and *The Black Album*, Meera Syal's *Anita and Me* (1996), Courttia Newland's *The Scholar* (1997)

and Diran Adebayo's *Some Kind of Black* (1996). You could also look at Courttia Newland and Kadija Sesay's anthology *IC3: The Penguin Book of New Black Writing in Britain* (2000), Onyekachi Wambu's *Empire Windrush: Fifty Years of Writing about Black Britain* (1998), or for a wider perspective, Kevin Powell's *Step into a World: A Global Anthology of the New Black Literature* (2000), which includes a contribution from Smith. For a non-fiction account of black immigrant experience in the U.K., Mike and Trevor Phillips' *Windrush: The Irresistible Rise of Multi-Racial Britain* (1998) is worth reading. Yasmin Alibhai-Brown has written extensively on the tensions and possibilities of a new multicultural Britain—see her *Who Do We Think We Are: Imagining the New Britain* (2000). Paul Gilroy's *"There Ain't No Black in the Union Jack": The Cultural Politics of Race and Nation* (1987) is an earlier work, but formative in thinking about the hopes for and failures of a multicultural Britain. Critical books on British multicultural writing include A Robert Lee's *Other Britain, Other British* (1995) and James Proctor's *Writing Black Britain 1948–1998: An Interdisciplinary Anthology* (2000).

Chance, Character, Gender, and Generation

16. The novel opens with Archie's failed suicide attempt. He is given a "second chance." How much of the plot is powered by chance, and how much by the motivations and beliefs of the characters? Archie often tosses a coin to make decisions. What does this reveal about his character? How does Samad's way of running his life differ? In what ways does this reflect on, and explain, their friendship?

17. Archie and Samad both marry women who are much younger than themselves, Archie after being rescued from his attempted

suicide, and Samad by his family's arrangement. How does the relationship between their wives develop? Consider the scene where the pregnant Clara and Alsana, and Alsana's "Niece-of-Shame," Neena, meet in the park (pp. 73–82). How does their friendship differ from Archie and Samad's? How are mothers and fathers represented in the novel (the Chalfens, as well as the Iqbals and the Joneses)?

18. After Samad sends Magid back to Bangladesh without consulting his wife, Alsana begins her long-running policy of "*exquisite* revenge," where she refuses to answer him directly. What other forms of resistance and conflict are there between the genders in *White Teeth*? Alsana and Samad's relationship is sometimes physically violent. How does Smith portray this domestic violence? What is your opinion of the scenes where they fight?

19. Archie and Samad meet in World War II. When they try to talk about their experiences to their families, however, the typical reaction is that the wives and children "feign [...] narcolepsy." Do the characters always find it impossible in *White Teeth* to communicate across the generations? What is the role of O'Connell's in Archie and Samad's retreat from gender and generational conflict? Are the struggles between gender and generations more or less important in the novel than the difficulties and possibilities in communicating across cultures?

20. Smith herself has made the criticism of novel that it "dances about on the page, performs itself, concerns itself with writerliness instead of people, and is cold." Do you agree? Are the characters fully-rounded, or stereotypes? Are some characters drawn with more sympathy than others? Do you agree with James Wood's criticism that the novel is "a curious shuffle of sympathy and distance, affiliation and divorce, brilliance and cartoonishness, astonishing maturity and ordinary puerility"?

Generally, which of the critics' responses do you find more valid?

Narrative and Genre

21. What is the genre of *White Teeth*? To what extent is it a comic novel, or a satire? The novel is very clearly set in real times and identifiable places, but can it be described as a realist narrative? There are elements of fantasy in the narrative, such as the coincidences between the lives of the separated Magid and Millat. These moments could be descried as "magic realism." Do you agree that this is a mode that Smith uses? (*The Oxford Companion to English Literature* (2000) defines magic realist stories as typically having "a strong narrative drive, in which the recognizably realistic mingles with the unexpected and the inexplicable, and in which elements of dream, fairy story, or mythology combine with the everyday, often in a mosaic or kaleidoscopic pattern of refraction and recurrence.")

22. *White Teeth* has multiple narrative strands that function in a non-linear manner, although many of the strands are drawn together at the end. Is Smith's handling of these multiple narratives successful? One of the greatest criticisms of the novel is that the ending is too forced, and its attempt to unite all the disparate elements and characters too farcical. Do you agree? Numerous Shakespeare comedies end in similar scenes of reconciliation. Do you think the ending of *White Teeth* works in the same way? How else might the novel have ended? In one of the last paragraphs, Smith writes that "the end is simply the beginning of an even longer story." How do the very final paragraphs resist a sense of an ending?

23. In the course of *White Teeth* are inserted various historical events, including the assassination of the Indian Prime Minister

Indira Gandhi in 1984, the hurricane that hit England in 1987, and *The Satanic Verses* affair in 1989. What is the function of these events in the narrative? Could *White Teeth* be described as a historical novel? Smith plays with notions of how history is constructed in *White Teeth*, with the ongoing argument about the place of Mangal Pande in Indian history, and with comic sections such as the timeline for *"The Post-War Reconstruction and Growth of O'Connell's Pool House."* What, then, is the relation of Smith's fiction to history?

Literary Influence

24. In interview, Smith has said that "The best, the only real training you can get is from reading other people's books." What evidence is there for Smith's own training in *White Teeth*? Which writers have influenced her work? Are there comparisons for Smith's work that have not been mentioned so far?

25. Smith has been critical of reviewers who have stated that her work draws on Salman Rushdie and Hanif Kureishi's writing. Her opinion is that just because her novel features non-white characters, it doesn't necessarily make them comparable to the characters in Rushdie and Kureishi. Do you think such comparisons are legitimate, or not? Is there a sense in which non-white writers are thought to be similar simply by virtue of not being white, or not writing about non-white characters? Are non-white writers expected to write about race issues, while white writers are not thought to be writing about their race?

The Literary Phenomenon

26. *White Teeth* has been an extraordinary success in both critical and commercial terms, as well as winning many prizes and

awards. Do you think this success is deserved? How much of the excitement about the book is to do with virtuosity of its writing, and how much to do with its subject matter or the youth and demographic profile of its author?

27. Is *White Teeth* a novel that should still be read and studied in ten years time, or fifty years time? Why? If so, what might it say to future readers about the period in which it was written?

BIBLIOGRAPHY

Works by Zadie Smith

Novels

White Teeth. London: Hamish Hamilton, 2000; New York: Random House, 2000.

Stories

"Mirrored Box", in Ruth Scurr and Chris Taylor, eds. *The May Anthology of Oxford and Cambridge Short Stories 1995* selected and introduced by John Holloway. Oxford and Cambridge: Varsity Publications Ltd and Cherwell (Oxford Student Publications Ltd), 1995. 125–141.

"The Newspaper Man", in Nick Laird and Toby Smith, eds. *The May Anthology of Oxford and Cambridge Short Stories 1996* selected and introduced by Penelope Fitzgerald. Oxford and Cambridge: Varsity Publications Ltd and Cherwell (Oxford Student Publications Ltd), 1996. 7–33.

"Mrs Begum's Son and the Private Tutor", in Martha Kelly, ed. *The May Anthology of Oxford and Cambridge Short Stories 1997* selected and introduced by Jill Paton Walsh. Oxford and Cambridge: Varsity Publications Ltd and Cherwell (Oxford Student Publications Ltd), 1997. 89–113.

"Picnic, Lightning", in Martha Kelly, ed. *The May Anthology of Oxford and Cambridge Short Stories 1997* selected and introduced by Jill Paton Walsh. Oxford and Cambridge: Varsity Publications Ltd and Cherwell (Oxford Student Publications Ltd), 1997. 115–122.

"The Waiter's Wife", in *Granta 67: Women and Children First*. Autumn 1999. 127–142.

"Stuart", in *The New Yorker*. 27 December 1999 and 3 January 2000. 60–67.

"I'm the Only One", in Nick Hornby, ed. *Speaking with the Angel*. London: Penguin, 2000. 79–89.

Miscellaneous

Introduction to *The May Anthologies 2001 Short Stories*. Cambridge: Varsity Publications Ltd, 2001.

Introduction to *Piece of Flesh*. London: Institute of Contemporary Arts, 2001.

Introduction to Lewis Carroll, *Through the Looking-Glass and What Alice Found There*, illustrated by Mervyn Peake. London: Bloomsbury, 2001.

Select Secondary Material

Criticism

Allardice, Lisa. "From Tangled Roots to Willesden Green". *Evening Standard*. 17 January 2000.

———. "Capital Gains". *The Times*. 20 January 2001.

Barnacle, Hugo. "The Highest Form of Flattery". *Sunday Times*. 23 January 2000.

Colin, Beatrice. "Not Enough Subject Matter To Really Sink Your Teeth Into". *Sunday Herald*. 23 January 2000.

Chisholm, Anne. "Post-racial conflicts". *Sunday Telegraph*. 16 January 2000.

Cryer, Dan. "In the Footsteps of Charles Dickens". *Newsday*. 8 May 2000.

Denes, Melissa. "The Sexiest Man in Cricklewood". *Daily Telegraph*. 15 January 2000.

Donahue, Deirdre. "'Teeth': A Knockout First Novel". *USA Today*. 27 April 2000.

Gamino, John. "Author Smith's Time Has Arrived". *Dallas Morning News*. 4 June 2000.

House, Christopher. "J Alfred Prufrock Meets Homer Simpson". *Independent*. 23 January 2000.

Iverem, Esther. "London Calling". *Washington Post*. 21 May 2000.

Jaggi, Maya. "In a Strange Land". *Guardian*. 22 January 2000.

Kakutani, Michiko. "*White Teeth*: Quirky, Sassy and Wise in a London of Exiles". *New York Times*. 25 April 2000.

Lanchester, John. "The Land of Accidents". *The New York Review of Books*. 8 February 2001.

Matthew, Christopher, and Anderson, Hephzibah. "Update: Fiction". *Daily Mail*. 21 January 2000.

Merritt, Stephanie. "Muslims in Willesden". *Literary Review*. February 2000.

Morris, Anne. "Zadie Smith's Zany '*White Teeth*'". *Austin American-Statesman*. 8 May 2000.

O'Connell, Alex. "Believe the Hype". *The Times*. 29 January 2000.

O'Rourke, Meghan. "Fiction in Review". *The Yale Review*. 2000, v.88: 3. 159–170.

Phillips, Caryl. "Mixed and Matched". *Observer*. 9 January 2000.

Quinn, Anthony. "The New England". *New York Times*. 30 April 2000.

Rozzo, Mark. "Who's English Now?". *Los Angeles Times*. 7 May 2000.

Sandhu, Sukhdev. "Excremental Children". *Times Literary Supplement*. 21 January 2000.

Smith, Ali. "Saga that goes straight to the heart of the century". *Scotsman*. 15 January 2000.

Soar, Daniel. "Willesden Fast-Forward". *London Review of Books*. 21 September 2000.

Tate, Greg. "Fear of a Mongrel Planet". *Village Voice*. 16 May 2000.

Vandenburgh, Jane. "Writing the Novel's Future". *Boston Globe*. 30 April 2000.

Wood, James. "Human, All Too Inhuman". *The New Republic*. 24 July 2000.

Interviews

Featherstone, Liza. "Talking with Zadie Smith". *Newsday*. 25 June 2000.

George, Lynell. "Author Purposeful with Prose, Fidgety with Fame". *Los Angeles Times*. 26 June 2000.

Hattenstone, Simon. "White Knuckle Ride". *Guardian*. 11 December 2000.

Jackson, Kevin. "Next Generation—Zadie Smith". *New Yorker*. 18 & 25 October 1999.

Jones, Vanessa E. "Grinding Her 'Teeth' ". *Boston Globe*. 13 June 2000.

Labi, Nadya. "Of Roots and Family Trees". *Time*. 22 May 2000.

Lyall, Sarah. "A Good Start". *New York Times*. 30 April 2000.

Merritt, Stephanie. "She's Young, Black, British—and the First Publishing Sensation of the Millennium". *Observer*. 16 January 2000.

Patterson, Christina. "Zadie Smith—A Willesden Ring Of Confidence". *Independent*. 22 January 2000.

Shelley, Jim. " 'I'm Not Going to the Orange Prize.' " *Mail on Sunday*. 7 May 2000.

Wallace, Sam. "Cutting her teeth with a book deal". *Daily Telegraph*. 15 January 2000.

Other Sources

Curtis, Nick. "Planet Cricklewood". *Evening Standard*. 6 June 2000.

Feay, Suzi. "Zadie Smith: More Than Just White Teeth". *Independent on Sunday*. 14 January 2001.

Gibbons, Fiachra. "The Route to Literary Success". *Guardian*. 28 March 2001.

Lewis, Miles Marshall. "The Black Book". *Village Voice*. 7 August 2001.

Sands, Sarah. "Zadie, the Woman Who Reinvented the Novelist". *Daily Telegraph*. 24 March 2000.

"Smith, Zadie". Clifford Thompson, ed. *Current Biography Yearbook 2000*. New York: The H. W. Wilson Company, 2000.

Websites

www.geocities.com/SoHo/Nook/1082/zadiesmithpage.html
www.salon.com/books/feature/2000/04/28/zadie/index.html
www.penguin.co.uk/static/packages/uk/articles/smith/smith.html (the U.K. publishers' website)
www.randomhouse.com/boldtype/0700/smith/ (the U.S. publishers' website)